THE 14TH DALAI LAMA

Aravinda has always loved books and stories and it seemed only natural that when she grew up, she too would write. She has had several jobs in dotcoms and other places. Her longest and most enjoyable stint has however been with a children's library called Hippocampus.

Aravinda is part of a small group called Think Tibet that organizes events to introduce people to the Tibetan community. For Think Tibet, Aravinda set up Lama Mani Books to publish Tibetan stories for children. She has authored two books, *Dorje's Holiday at the Gyenso Khang* and *Dolma Visits the City* (2009).

Aravinda lives in Bangalore with her husband, dog and a visiting menagerie of dogs, squirrels, crows and snails.

Other books in the *Puffin Lives* series

THE 14TH
Dalai Lama

BUDDHA OF
COMPASSION

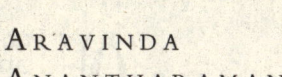

ARAVINDA
ANANTHARAMAN

PUFFIN BOOKS

An imprint of Penguin Random House

PUFFIN BOOKS

USA | Canada | UK | Ireland | Australia
New Zealand | India | South Africa | China | Singapore

Puffin Books is part of the Penguin Random House group of companies
whose addresses can be found at global.penguinrandomhouse.com

Published by Penguin Random House India Pvt. Ltd
4th Floor, Capital Tower 1, MG Road,
Gurugram 122 002, Haryana, India

First published in Puffin by Penguin Books India 2011

Copyright © Aravinda Anantharaman 2011

All rights reserved

10 9 8 7 6 5 4 3 2

ISBN 9780143331834

Typeset in Bembo by Eleven Arts, New Delhi
Printed at Repro India Limited

www.penguin.co.in

For Amma and Appa

Acknowledgements

I'd like to acknowledge the Tibetan community in exile for sharing their stories over the years, and my friends at Think Tibet, Tenzin Jangchup and Lobsang Thardoe for helping keep these stories alive. Thanks also to the Office of His Holiness the Dalai Lama, Claude Arpi, Glenn Mullin, Thomas Laird, the Nobel Foundation, Aitken Alexander Associates, Srishti Publishers & Distributors and Friends of Tibet for permissions. A special thanks to my publishers, Puffin Books, and especially my editors Mimi Basu and Sohini Mitra for making the story even better than what it was when it began.

Contents

1 The Chosen One

Four-year old Lhamo Dhondup sat on the ornate high throne. Dressed in heavy ceremonial robes, he surveyed the crowds that thronged to the palace. His eyes searched for familiar faces and finally found them in the front row, looking up at him. His mother, Deki Tsering, his father, Choekyong Tsering, his older sister Tsering Dolma and his three older brothers, Thubten Jigme Norbu, Gyalo Dhondup and Lobsang Samten. Already, there was distance between them—he could not jump up and run to his mother, as he would have liked to very much. His family must have felt the same. Lobsang Samten, closest to Lhamo in age and his constant playmate, looked indignant at not being allowed to sit up on the throne with his kid brother.

In the palace, dignitaries from far and wide stood respectfully while high officials conducted the coronation ceremony. Everyone had brought presents—horses, cattle, gold, silver, precious stones and rare manuscripts— for the boy chosen as the 14th Dalai Lama of Tibet. Lhamo looked at his gifts with growing boredom. And then something caught his fancy—a Meccano model construction set gifted by the British representative, who must have realized that he may be no less than the Dalai Lama was only a boy.

In Lhasa, there was jubilation that the seat of the Dalai Lama, which had been empty for seven long years was occupied once more. The Regent* rejoiced because his long search for the incarnation of his master, the 13th Dalai Lama had finally come to an end. Lhamo's family felt honoured and blessed that the highest incarnation in Tibet had chosen their humble home to be born into. And as for Lhamo, he looked forward to playing with his Meccano set. It stirred his interest in all things mechanical, and growing up as the Dalai Lama of Tibet, one of his favourite pastimes was to take machines apart to see how they worked. And putting them together again with the hope that they would still work.

Lhamo's birth had been eventful. It is believed that the village where an important monk will incarnate will see misfortune for a few years before the birth. And so it was with Taktser village in the province of Amdo. For several months before Lhamo Dhondup was born, the village experienced many disasters, including long seasons of drought. There were hailstorms too, and much livestock was lost. People wondered at the strange turn of events: Could it be that all this was pointing towards the birth of someone important? Or were they merely paying the price for their sins? The family of Choekyong

---

* High ranking monk traditionally chosen to govern the country till the Dalai Lama reached the maturity to rule alone.

Tsering, too, suffered considerably and the master of the house himself lay on his deathbed.

It was in the month of July, 1935 and the rains lashed outside as Deki gave birth to a boy. At the same time as the child was born, Choekyong found himself miraculously cured of all his afflictions. Outside, the weather cleared and a rainbow had appeared in the sky. The villagers came to Choekyong's house to see this special child who had brought good fortune to Taktser. He was named Lhamo Dhondup, which means 'wish-fulfilling goddess'. Choekyong, was so relieved at things changing for the better, that he named his son after the goddess Palden Lhamo, who is considered an important goddess in the pantheon of Tibetan deities.

When Lhamo was two years old, a group of travellers stopped at his house one day. This was a common practice in Tibet, where in the absence of hotels and restaurants, travellers would often stop for shelter and meals at people's homes. Deki welcomed the weary travellers warmly. Lhamo, curious and not at all shy, walked over to one of the servants, a smiling man with kind eyes, who was accompanying the travellers. Settling on his lap, Lhamo's little hands reached for the rosary around the servant's neck, and he asked for it.

'I'll give it to you if you tell me who I am,' said the servant.

'You are Sera-aga,' answered the boy. A monk from Sera monastery.

'And who is that?' asked the servant, pointing to the master.

'That is Losang,' replied the boy.

Looking pleased, the servant, who was actually a senior monk named Kesang in disguise, removed his rosary and handed it to Lhamo. He then spent the rest of the day watching the boy play. The next morning, the travellers set off on their journey. And to Deki's surprise, Lhamo ran behind them crying that he too be allowed to go with them.

A few weeks later a group of monks came to their home. They were dressed in robes that indicated their high rank and importance. They asked for Lhamo. In Tibet, it is not uncommon to hear of rebirths and this is especially true of monks and holy people. So, when Choekyong and Deki saw this entourage of monks at their doorsteps they suspected that perhaps their son Lhamo was a reincarnation of a senior monk from the Kumbum monastery, which was near Taktser. He had passed away recently and the couple assumed that this was the search party.

The monks laid out a few objects—two black rosaries, two yellow rosaries and two walking sticks. Lhamo was asked to choose one of each. As he walked around selecting the rosaries and the walking stick, the monks exchanged relieved and joyous looks. When he had picked up the last of the three objects, they knelt down and bowed to him, 'Kundun.'

Choekyong and Deki were speechless. Their son, Lhamo, was the Kundun? The Dalai Lama!

It seemed difficult to believe and yet, here were the great monks from Lhasa who believed that the search for the 14th incarnation of the Dalai Lama had ended in a peasant's home in Taktser. For four long years, the Regent had been seeking the boy who would one day govern Tibet again. The signs had pointed in the northeastern direction. The Regent had even travelled to the lake of Lhamoi Lhatso and meditated there for direction. This was the sacred lake of the deity Palden Lhamo, who as tradition has it had promised the first Dalai Lama to watch over his successors The vision that appeared revealed the syllables *Ah, Ka, Ma,* a house with turquoise tiles on the roof, very like the one Lhamo lived in, and a monastery with jade and gold rooftops in the vicinity. Later, they deduced that *Ah* meant Amdo and *Ka* must refer to Kumbum monastery. And true to the signs, the reincarnation had been found.

Other marks of the Dalai Lama included physical features like tiger stripes on the legs, wide-set eyes, large ears, two fleshy outgrowths on the shoulder blades and a conch shell imprint on the palm of the hand. Later, these were also found on Lhamo Dhondup.

While arrangements were being made to take Lhamo Dhondup to Lhasa, he could not be permitted to continue living at home with his parents and was hence sent to the Kumbum monastery. Lobsang Samten, his immediate elder brother, accompanied Lhamo and the two were left under the care of their uncle. At Kumbum, the boys had a great time, getting into trouble often.

Once Lhamo found a set of palm-leaf scriptures and managed to mess them up completely. His uncle was livid and slapped the boy. On occasions when they had angered their uncle, which was fairly often, Lhamo and Lobsang would hide from him for hours on end. From under cover, they would hear their uncle search for them, growing increasingly frantic. The brothers were too young to realize the extent of the responsibility that had been placed on him and the stress of ensuring the new Dalai Lama's safety. Young that they were, they did what boys did—get into trouble and then hide from it.

The brothers stayed at Kumbum for two years, oblivious of the changes which lay ahead. As the Dalai Lama, Lhamo was required to reside in Lhasa, the capital city that lay at the far end of Tibet, closer to the borders of Nepal and Bhutan. When the arrangements were completed, preparations were made to begin the journey to Lhasa. Lhamo's family decided to move with him, leaving behind their home and their life as peasants. Lhamo's journey to his destiny was just beginning.

The journey to Lhasa

Amdo being on the north-eastern border was under Chinese rule and the governor was a warlord named Ma Pu Feng. He had not been informed that the Dalai Lama's reincarnation had been found. Instead, the search party had merely told him that they were here to look for suitable candidates for the reincarnation. When Lhamo Dhondup was presented as the most likely candidate, Ma Pu Feng demanded an enormous sum as the price to let the boy leave Amdo. When the payment was made, he demanded yet more. And so it was that for two years, Lhamo Dhondup had to stay in Amdo while negotiations continued. It was never let out that he had been confirmed as the reincarnation.

The journey from Amdo to Lhasa began in July 1939 and took three months and thirteen days. The entourage was made up of fifty people including Lhamo's parents, two of his brothers, the members of the search party, Muslim pilgrims, Chinese escorts and guides. There were 350 horses and many mules to make the journey possible. For Lhamo, a special carriage was strapped on the backs of two mules. He and Lobsang Samten travelled in it. The terrain was difficult as there were no proper roads. Every day, the group travelled from dawn to noon.

In Lhasa, the officials waited. As soon as news arrived that the group had crossed the area of Chinese control, they made the formal declaration that the next reincarnation had been found. High officials then left Lhasa to meet the new Dalai Lama on the way.

Just outside of Lhasa, the officials met the travellers. A tent was erected and a symbolic offering called *Mendel Tensum** was made and Lhamo Dhondup was officially proclaimed as the 14th Dalai Lama. His peasant clothes were replaced with ceremonial robes. From this point on, he rode in a golden carriage, alone.

The road to Lhasa was lined with people who had

---

* A traditional offering consisting of a golden figure of Buddha, a book of scriptures about Buddha and about the Dalai Lama's duty to propagate Buddhism, and a miniature container containing a holy relic.

gathered to see the new reincarnation. Dressed in finery they thronged the streets waiting for a glimpse of their new ruler. Looking out of his carriage, the Dalai Lama saw people crying with joy. Their Kundun had returned.

Even as the festivities continued outside the city, Lhamo Dhondup was taken to the Norbulingka or 'The Jewelled Park', the traditional summer residence of the Dalai Lamas, located west of Lhasa.

The procession to the Potala Palace

The coronation procession took place a few months later, on 22 February 1940. It was a holiday that the people of Tibet looked forward to. They thronged the streets of Lhasa to welcome the Dalai Lama's return to his seat, the Potala Palace.

The procession was a grand ceremony and took place over several hours. The entourage was large and colourful in its royal attire. At the head were the servants dressed in green tunics, blue breeches and red tasselled hats. They carried the personal belongings of the Dalai Lama. Behind them came the grooms and attendants holding banners, to ward off evil. Then came the high lamas, the State Oracle, politicians and other delegates. Right after them were the men who led the Dalai Lama's ponies. The head monks of the Potala in their maroon robes came next, followed by the lay officials in order of rank. The Potala was located on a hill, and to navigate the incline, two rows of men in green uniforms, wearing read hats with white plumes, followed carrying draw ropes. And it took six bearers to carry the yoke of the Dalai Lama's golden palanquin, which was flanked by two umbrellas, one golden, the colour associated with the Dalai Lama, and the other green, Lhamo Dhondup's lucky shade.

Behind the Kundun's palanquin followed his Regent, Reting Rinpoche. His parents and brothers came next followed by Abbots along with *tulkus* or reincarnate lamas. Other monks and officials made up the rear of the group that grew in size as spectators joined it. Inside the Potala, Kundun was lifted onto the Lion Throne and the ceremony began.

Tibet and the Dalai Lamas

Snug in the mountains, the country Tibet was not familiar to the world. Few travellers wandered so high up in the Himalayas. And fewer still came into Tibet. And yet, strange though it may seem, the teachings of the Buddha reached this country of nomads and peasants and yaks. Here, it flourished in the Mahayana tradition, borrowing characteristics from the existing religion of Bön, and becoming what would eventually be known the world over as Tibetan Buddhism.

Spirituality is revered in Tibet. Tibetans believe in rebirth and use their lives wisely and carefully. The practice of Buddhism is an important aspect of their life. Earlier almost every family sent a child to the monastery. The role of religion was visible in everything Tibetans did. Hundreds of prayer flags would flutter in the wind, stones inscribed with prayers would line the roadside, several monasteries thrived across the country, and people spent days in prayer. The role of deities and enlightened beings was unquestioned.

Tibetans believe that the Dalai Lama is the reincarnation of Avalokiteshwara or Chenrezig, the Buddha of Compassion. The story goes that Chenrezig could not bear to see people suffer and vowed to be born again and again until all suffering ceased. And so his incarnations return after every lifetime to continue his work. The first incarnation was Gedun Drupa. The term 'Dalai Lama' was given to the third incarnation by a Mongol king and it has become almost the title for this incarnation of Chenrezig. The lineage has followed the path of reincarnation, a phenomenon that is not at all uncommon in Tibetan Buddhism. Among the incarnations, the fifth and the thirteenth occupy a significant place in Tibet's history. Tibet, during the time of the fifth Dalai Lama, saw a period of political upheaval and he took over the reigns of rule. From then on, the successive Dalai Lamas have been the heads of state. The current Dalai Lama is the fourteenth incarnation.

2   Growing Up as the Dalai Lama

As the incarnation of the Dalai Lama, Lhamo was ordained as a monk and given a new name, Jamphel Ngawang Lobsang Yeshe Tenzin Gyatso. It translates as Holy One, Tender Glory, Mighty in Speech, Compassionate One, Defender of the Faith, Ocean of Wisdom. For the people of Tibet, he was simply their 'Kundun' or the Presence and that is how everyone, including his family, addressed him. Later in life, he used the last two names Tenzin Gyatso for his official signature.

In Lhasa, the Dalai Lama lived in two palaces—the grand and imposing Potala Palace, the official residence, and the smaller but more welcoming Norbulingka, the summer palace. For half the year, the Potala was Kundun's home. It was built over a thousand years ago by a Tibetan King as a place for meditation. When the 5th Dalai Lama was in power, he began the expansion of the Potala. This was around the same time that the Taj Mahal was built in India. Perhaps if Tibet had been more accessible to the world, the Potala may have been in the running for one of the wonders of the world, for what a palace it is!

The Potala is almost a city in itself, covering the entire top of Lhasa's Red Hill. The colours of the Potala are dark red and white—the red portion housing the school and the prayer halls, and the areas painted in white containing the residence of the Dalai Lama and the offices. In the Potala lived hundreds of monks besides the Dalai Lama. Within the palace were also enclosed a school, many chapels, libraries, offices, storerooms and, of course, the mausoleums of some of the past Dalai Lamas. Kundun's rooms lay at 400 feet above the town of Lhasa, and here he lived with his brother Lobsang Samten.

Life as the Dalai Lama had its advantages and disadvantages. The daily routine of Kundun was so packed with lessons that he barely left the palace. And even if he did, it was only for official purposes, and therefore with a complete retinue of officials, teachers and bodyguards. Kundun's family were given an estate in Lhasa and he did visit them every few weeks, but otherwise, the Potala was his world. On the positive side, the palace was so large that Lobsang Samten and Kundun spent many hours exploring the various rooms and stumbling upon unexpected treasures. They especially enjoyed rummaging through the possessions of the 13th Dalai Lama.

Why did Lhamo Dhondup have to become a monk?

Tibetan Buddhism follows a strong monastic tradition, which focuses on the practice of Buddhist scriptures. One theory is that when Buddhism reached Tibet, the religion that already was in practice there was Bön. The new faith absorbed many of the existing practices and hence Tibetan Buddhism assumed a form that is unique and different from Buddhist customs elsewhere. The monastic tradition is integral to both Bön and Tibetan Buddhist traditions.

Second, the lineage of the Dalai Lama is a monastic one. As a reincarnation of a monk, the Dalai Lamas are all ordained as one; with the exception of the 6th Dalai Lama who chose to remain a layman and was given the privilege to do so.

When Kundun was aged six, his studies began. The major subjects he was coached in were logic, Tibetan art and culture, Sanskrit, medicine, and Buddhist philosophy. The five minor subjects he learnt were poetry, music and drama, astrology, phrasing, and synonyms. The Regent was his Senior Tutor. He also had a Junior Tutor, Taktra Rinpoche, and three other monk-officials to assist him—the Master of Rituals, the Master of Robes and the Master of the Kitchens. The Master of the Kitchens, Lobsang Jinpa, became Kundun's favourite. Kundun affectionately called him Ponpo.

Kundun's daily routine:

6 a.m.: Wake up

6–7 a.m.: Prayer and meditation

7 a.m.: Breakfast (usually the Tibetan staple dish, *tsampa,* which is made with roasted barley flour and moistened with some butter tea, a popular drink made with tea leaves, yak butter and salt)

8–10 a.m.: Penmanship or practising writing, and memorization of scriptures
10 a.m.: Meeting with members of the government
Until noon: Lessons in scriptures with the Junior Tutor
12 noon to 1 p.m.: Playtime
1 p.m.: Lunch
2 p.m.–4 p.m.: More lessons with Junior Tutor
4 p.m.: Tea
4:15–5:30 p.m.: Debating practice
5:30 p.m.: Lessons for the day are over
7 p.m.: Dinner
9 p.m.: Bedtime

Kundun was still so young. He missed his family, especially his mother and she obviously did too. She would try and visit her son at the palace, often hiding his favourite foods that she would furtively slip to him. Although the monks were not strict vegetarians, there were some kinds of food like eggs and pork that they frowned upon. And Kundun as a boy had a particular fondness for them. Once, when he was enjoying some boiled eggs, a senior official happened to see him. Both the official and Kundun were horrified. Kundun reacted first, 'Go away,' he shouted.

Around this time, a younger brother was born to Kundun and a few years later, a younger sister. The family was now made of two girls and five boys, including Kundun. But keeping him company in his 'golden prison' were Lobsang Samten and Ponpo. Besides them,

Kundun's playmates were the sweepers of the palace who wholeheartedly joined him in his pranks.

And what a prankster he could be! One of Kundun's earliest public appearances was at the Monlam or the Great Prayer Festival. This is an important date in the Tibetan calendar, celebrated with pomp and festivities. The Jokhang Temple at Lhasa was the venue for the celebrations and Kundun was dressed in his best finery and taken there to initiate the celebrations. While at Jokhang, his tutors forbade him from running to the window and looking out. He was after all the Dalai Lama. So, naturally, Kundun found the idea irresistible. When no one was watching, he leaned out of the nearest window and peered down. Seeing their Kundun looking out, the people rushed to the walls of the Jokhang and began prostrating before the God-King. God-King or not, he was still a boy who proceeded to blow spit bubbles which fell on the heads of the gathering!

His tutors, however, were not always indulgent of his pranks. They treated their young ward with strict discipline and Kundun remembers the two whips that hung on the walls of the school room—one was for Lobsang Samten, and a special yellow one was the 'holy' whip, reserved for the Dalai Lama. And whenever the boys were too naughty, the sight of the whip was enough to keep them in check.

Grand and imposing though the Potala was, it was the Norbulingka or the summer palace that Kundun preferred. Built by the 7th Dalai Lama, it had several orchards and gardens. Shifting from the Potala to the Norbulingka was an event marked with colour and gaiety and everyone looked forward to it. For Kundun, the Norbulingka proffered a freedom that the Potala did not. At Norbulingka, there were willow, juniper and poplar trees. There were also peacocks and musk deer, some mountain goats, camels from Mongolia, a couple of leopards and even an old tiger! And so many birds too—geese and parrots and cranes! The Norbulingka was built around a lake and Kundun loved to feed the fish. Later, he recalled that as soon as the fish heard his footsteps, they would rise near the edge expectantly.

An even bigger attraction that the Norbulingka held for Kundun was the availability of three cars, the only ones in all of Tibet. There were two Baby Austins, and a Dodge. Kundun, not surprisingly, began tinkering with all three cars. The Baby Austins had not been used for long and refused to start. With the help of Tashi Tsering, his driver, he did manage to get one of the cars working. Now, Kundun had been forbidden to drive the cars and so naturally, he decided to try it out one night. He chose the Baby Austin, took the wheel and crashed into a nearby tree, breaking one of the headlights. Guiltily, he tried to quickly make a replacement for it. He used sugar syrup to recreate the tinted effect and hoped the short-tempered Tashi Tsering would not notice. To his credit, Tashi Tsering, perhaps more amused than angry, pretended not to detect the damage the next morning and the incident went unreported.

Kundun also tinkered with everything he got his hands on—an old generator, watches, toys . . .

His natural curiosity and interest in the world around him grew with age. And in his explorations, the Potala did not disappoint. It consistently threw up treasures, most of which were gifts given to the 13th Dalai Lama that had been carefully stored away.

One day deep in the recesses of the Potala, Kundun and Lobsang Samten came across an old projector. Further exploration led to their unearthing thirty reels of film. The boys had never seen anything like this before! From among the great many monks who lived in the Potala, it seemed there was one who had been living there since the time of the 13th Dalai Lama, and who knew how to set up the projector and film. And that's how Kundun came to watch over and over again with much interest the few films that he had got his hands upon: a documentary on gold mining, footage on the Boer War in South Africa, a film on King George V, another one on Tarzan and a rather bizarre film on trick photography.

Watches were another weakness of Kundun's. For a long time he carried the 13th Dalai Lama's pocket watch but it was wristwatches that he found irresistible. Soon enough, he acquired a Rolex and an Omega watch from the Lhasa market. One of the first things he did with his acquisitions was to open them out to see what made the hands move. He soon became adept at repairing watches.

In 1943, at the age of seven, he acquired a Patek Philippe, a gift from the US President Roosevelt.

The Second World War was then at its height and the American President sent two envoys to Lhasa as he wanted to build a road between India and China through Tibet. The two emissaries were Ilia Tolstoy, the grandson of famed Russian author Leo Tolstoy, and Brooke Dolan, a renowned naturalist. The envoys carried a letter from the President and the gift of a Patek Philippe's newest model gold watch. Kundun loved the present and despite the several repairs the watch has needed, it remains in working condition even today.

How life changed for Lhamo Dhondup's family after he became Kundun

Lhamo Dhondup's family lived as simple peasants in the village of Taktser. They had lived here for generations. Their home was a single-storeyed house that faced the Mountain Amichiri. As with other traditional families, there was a pole in the middle of the courtyard from which prayer flags fluttered. The family owned a Tibetan mastiff dog, and their livestock included eight cows, seven *dzomos* (the female of a yak and cow), and some chickens.

The day began at dawn and with the lighting of the lamps at the altar. Lhamo's mother Deki would then make butter tea, which is a perennial favourite in Tibet. People drink several cups of this beverage through the day and it is perfect for the weather. Choekyong Tsering had a prized collection of horses that he would take

special care of. The family lived on agriculture mainly, and most of the day was spent in farming. In the evenings, Choekyong Tsering would again tend to his horses while his wife milked the cows. Dinner was usually *tsampa* and vegetables in the summer and *tsampa* and *thukpa* (noodle soup) in winter. Meat was a rarity.

As the father of the Dalai Lama, Choekyong Tsering's position elevated to that of a nobleman. The family moved to Lhasa. No longer peasants, they had to adapt to the new ways, a new city and a new lifestyle. Even the language was something to learn as they spoke a dialect that was specific to the Amdo border and quite unlike the Lhasan Tibetan. In Lhasa, Choekyong Tsering participated in the morning meetings at the Potala. However, he still maintained his stable, perhaps his greatest passion. Despite the change of lifestyle and the prosperity that surrounded them, it was Kundun's mother, Deki Tsering who held her family together with her down-to-earth attitude. She was, Kundun says, a woman who was incredibly kind. The fact that they were now noblemen and Tibet's first family did not change her. She seldom displayed any pretensions to aristocracy. Deki Tsering, in her autobiography *Dalai Lama, My Son* writes: 'Though great honor had now become my fate, I wept inside for my home. There I had to work hard ... but I had been at peace and extremely happy. I had had freedom and privacy. Now I was treated like a queen, but I was not as happy.'

3   The World on the Other Side of the Mountain

Shangri-La is a fictional place that was described in the novel *Lost Horizon* written by James Hilton in 1933. It is a paradise of sorts, a permanently happy land hidden in the Himalayan mountains and isolated from the rest of the world. It is now used as a metaphor while speaking of a place that is not unlike what Hilton wrote about.

There are but a few accounts of travellers tales about Tibet. For long, it was the Shangri-La, the paradise, high in the mountains. It was a country of religious people and monks who, if stories are to be believed, had superhuman powers. It was a country of great riches. It was also a country of people who were not interested in the world beyond their own. Tibet, for long, had closeted herself from the rest of the globe. The people were happy with their existence, and contact with the rest of the world was limited to traders who came to Nepal or Sikkim in order to barter salt and wool. Only a few people from outside had ever visited Tibet. And even then, most accounts by travellers dwell only on life in Lhasa.

In Tibet there are three main provinces—Amdo which is the north-eastern region of Tibet, Kham which spans the region between the north-west and south-east borders, and U–Tsang which is Central Tibet. Lhasa lies in the U–Tsang province at an elevation of around 3500m. Now, Lhasa is a large settlement, the capital city, habited by high officials, feudal lords and the like. The way of life here is marked by a rich and easy way of living with celebrations, festivities, excessive eating and drinking. The rest of Tibet, however is far different. Here, people are either nomads who graze their cattle or farmers who till the land. Their survival depends on hard work. There are no weekends, and the one holiday they permit themselves is Losar or the New Year. Indeed, most Tibetans have not ventured so far towards Lhasa or even set their eyes on the place. It was the rare few who had made the pilgrimage to this holy city, the seat of the Kundun.

Kundun and his seeing eye

In Lhasa, Kundun's natural curiosity drew him to see the world around him, for himself. Among the Great Thirteenth's possessions was a telescope, and this became one of Kundun's absolute favourites. He set it up on the Potala's terrace and spent much of his free time looking through it. Perhaps it offered him an introduction to a more worldly and scientific view that his religious teachings did not.

More importantly, the telescope brought him a view of reality that he was otherwise shielded from. He followed the lives of people in the city outside, in the markets and even in the prison. Especially the prison.

Every evening, when his lessons for the day were over, Kundun rushed to the terrace of the Potala to his telescope. He usually focused it on the prison at the foot of the hill. This was the time of day when the inmates were allowed to walk about in the yard and Kundun observed them through his telescope.

In his autobiography, *Freedom in Exile,* Kundun writes, 'I considered them to be my friends and kept a close eye on their movements. They knew this and whenever they caught sight of me threw themselves in prostration. I recognized them all and always knew when someone was released and there was a new arrival.'

Sometimes he trained the telescope on people's houses. He saw the parties, the gaiety and the merriment. When people realized that they were being watched by their Kundun, they would hide away, sometimes out of shame but mostly because they understood that he would never experience the life they led, and felt a little sorry for that.

With the years, Kundun also became increasingly aware of the world outside Tibet. These were times of great changes all over; the Second World War ended when Kundun was ten years old. In Asia itself, most of the subcontinent had for so long been under colonial occupation that things were coming to a head. China, Tibet's closest neighbour, was at war with Japan. This was followed by the Communist Party's rise to power and the formation of the People's Republic of China. Kundun followed the news of the outside world with growing curiosity. A Tibetan newspaper, *Sargyur Melong,* was published once a month in Kalimpong, India. Kundun read it with interest. He read about the war, he saw pictures in the magazine, *Life*, that people brought him. And increasingly, like his predecessor, he too was beginning to feel that Tibet could no longer remain isolated from the rest of the world. She had to seek friends and build alliances both with neighbours and with the powers which were afar.

How had the 13th Dalai Lama tried to break the isolation that Tibet was in?

It was not only Kundun who thought that Tibet needed to be modernized. His predecessor, the 13th Dalai Lama, Thupten Gyatso, had also worked towards this. Thupten Gyatso, or the Great Thirteenth as he is referred to, governed Tibet between 1895 and 1933. Almost single-handedly, he took on the mission to pull Tibet out from her self-imposed isolation and set her on the path to modernization.

When the 13th Dalai Lama assumed power, he realized that Tibet could not and should not remain in seclusion. Alliances and strategic collaborations were necessary to keep the Chinese away from Tibet's borders. Twice, the Great Thirteenth had to escape into exile due to Chinese invasions. The first time, he went to Mongolia and the second time, to Darjeeling where he stayed for two years. However, through these political fluctuations, the 13th Dalai Lama actively pursued international relations, meeting diplomats from various counties: Britain, the United States, Russia and France. He also reached out to his neighbours in Mongolia, Nepal, and Sikkim urging them to defend their independence, because he recognized that the threat from China was real.

In trying to build an independent state, the Great Thirteenth went on to create a national flag for Tibet, and a national anthem. He also had postal stamps and bank notes issued. Modernization in Tibet found a beginning with the Great Thirteenth. Along with this, he tried to discard certain old customs that no longer made sense in the present day. For instance, every time the Dalai Lama came out of his chambers, his servants were expected to step away out of sight. The Great Thirteenth said this made him reluctant to come out and asked that this practice be stopped. On the outside, he introduced a lot of excitement when he bought three motorcars. A road was paved in Lhasa for the cars. The story goes that every winter, the entourage left the Norbulingka for Potala as was tradition. The Great Thirteenth didn't like the Potala very much but agreed to keep up the ritual by being a part of the grand procession. But on reaching the Potala and once the ceremonies were over and the crowds had dispersed, he would get into his car and drive right back to the Norbulingka! The Great Thirteenth is also credited with introducing electricity and telephone in Tibet. He also set up an English school in Gyantse, and arranged for four Tibetan boys to be educated in Britain. The idea was that they would be exposed to modern education and progressive thinking and on their return this would be of immense value to Tibetans. He even created a police force in Tibet.

The Great Thirteenth was thus trying to revolutionize several areas, in education, health, politics and international relations when he died. In more ways than one, Kundun's predecessor had already pointed him the direction he was to take—the other side of the mountain.

4 An Unusual Friendship

Kundun and Lobsang Samten were close companions but like brothers anywhere in the world, they fought incessantly. Finally, the monks resolved to send Lobsang Samten away for a few years. It was a decision that neither of the two boys were happy with, but they had no say in the matter. With Lobsang away, Kundun really had no one his age for company in the palace. After a few years though Lobsang Samten returned and continued his life at the Potala.

Around this time, Tibet was still an isolated country and there were only six foreigners living here—a missionary and two radio operators who were British, a Belarusian prisoner of war and two Austrian prisoners of war who had reached Tibet after the war ended. Their names were Heinrich Harrer and Peter Aufschnaiter.

Looking through his telescope, Kundun often caught sight of the blond Harrer walking on the streets of Lhasa. Of course, Harrer did not know about this for a long time.

Harrer had been part of a mountaineering expedition to the Nanga Parbat peak, led by Peter Aufschnaiter. After the expedition the group returned to Karachi. This was August 1939. To their ill luck, the Second

World War was declared two days later in Europe. Finding themselves in a British 'enemy' colony, Peter Aufschnaiter, Heinrich Harrer and two others were arrested within hours. They were now prisoners of war. After several attempts to escape, Harrer and Aufschnaiter managed to break out and made their way towards Tibet. Aufschnaiter was familiar with the region, knew the language and so it was their best bet. They reached Tibet in January 1946, after the war had ended, and slowly made their way to Lhasa.

Harrer was a person of many skills, a man who had studied Geography and Sports at university, had qualified for skiing competitions and had scaled peaks in Europe. One of his areas of expertise was ice-skating. He began teaching some of the Tibetans to skate over a frozen lake. One of his pupils was Lobsang Samten. When Lobsang tried to describe this wonderful sport of 'walking on knives' to his brother, Kundun was fascinated. The next day he turned his telescope in the direction of the frozen lake but unfortunately, it was too far away and hence not visible to him. He could not go out and see for himself, much as he would have liked to. Shortly after, Lobsang Samten went for his skating lessons one day carrying a film recorder in his hands and a request from Kundun to record the boys skating. Kundun had also thoughtfully sent along the instruction manual and Harrer, who was skilled in engineering but had never filmed anything before, agreed to try. After studying the manual, he filmed the group skating. The film was then sent to India to be developed. It was two months before Kundun could view the movie and he was delighted with what he saw! This was the beginning of a close association. Harrer was called upon to record several important events in Lhasa during his stay there. And he did so gladly. But he had never yet met the God-King of Tibet. All requests were sent through Lobsang Samten or other officials and, in turn, Harrer responded through the same means.

One day, Lobsang Samten came to Harrer with a more ambitious suggestion from Kundun: 'Would Mr Harrer build a film room at the Norbulingka?' Now Harrer and Peter Aufschnaiter had already been making themselves useful in Lhasa with their various skills in engineering, cartography or map making, ice-skating and whatnot. There was no saying 'No', especially to the Dalai Lama.

Harrer set about constructing a room for viewing films and this took months. One day shortly after the room had been readied, Harrer was riding outside the city when he was called to stop by one of Kundun's bodyguards. The guard came bearing an urgent message asking Harrer to report to the Norbulingka. Harrer assumed that something had gone terribly wrong with the film room and rode back quickly. At the palace entrance, he was hurried inside by some monks. Harrer stepped past the wall that separated Kundun's private chambers from the rest of the palace. Just outside the new film room, Lobsang Samten stood waiting impatiently. As soon as he caught sight of Harrer, he thrust a white scarf, the *khata*, into the Austrian's hands and whispered in his ears, 'Kundun will see you now.'

In an unprecedented turn of events, the eleven-year old Dalai Lama of Tibet had decided to bypass protocol and invite his guest directly. Harrer presented the *khata* to Kundun. It was the first time that the two were meeting and Kundun had called him over so that they could together inaugurate the new camera and the room. His teachers disapproved, of course, but for Kundun, this seemed like a natural way of expressing his appreciation.

From that time on, Harrer was a regular visitor to the palace. He became Kundun's unofficial tutor, teaching him about the world. What Kundun had so far tried to glean from books and magazines, he now had someone to learn from. Geography, English, Current Affairs . . . Harrer brought these closer to Kundun. The boy was curious and asked a great many questions. And Harrer kept up as well as he could. Often their lessons went in all directions because of the questions Kundun had. They were on jet planes, atom bombs, rotation and revolution . . . just about anything.

Kundun's monastic learning focused on spirituality and philosophy, but as a future leader of his people, his instincts prompted him to seek knowledge about the reality of science and politics. In Harrer, Kundun met someone who not only possessed a deep love for Tibet but one who had wide-ranging interests and a tremendous sense of humour. In return, Harrer had found the best student he could have ever had—inquisitive, interested and with an understanding that belied his age.

Harrer left Tibet in 1950. He writes in his book *Seven Years in Tibet* that as his boat went down the river, his eyes remained glued on the Potala for he knew that his young friend was in there looking down at him through his telescope.

What became of Peter Aufschnaiter?

Peter Aufschnaiter's story is as interesting as Heinrich Harrer's, but little has been told and heard about him. Like Harrer, Peter too was an adventurer and loved the mountains.

Once they had reached Lhasa, Harrer and Aufschnaiter's lives began to gradually go separate ways. Peter was an agricultural engineer and a cartographer. Some time after their arrival in Lhasa, some senior officials summoned Peter and commissioned him to build an irrigation canal in the city. During his work on building the canal, he came across many pieces of vases, jugs, bowls, and even skeletons! All of these later became important archaeological evidence for the study of Tibetan history.

While engaged in their individual pursuits, Aufschnaiter and Harrer kept in touch throughout their stay in Lhasa. Following the Chinese invasion in 1950, Harrer chose to leave Tibet. On his journey out, he met Aufschnaiter in the Tibetan town of Gyantse. Though

Harrer had decided to leave Tibet for India under the changed political scenario, Aufschnaiter, chose to remain in the country.

After this meeting Harrer reports that there was no news of Aufschnaiter for a long time. He was feared dead. Peter Aufschnaiter, however, did not die; he made his way back to a place called Kyirong in southern Tibet that both men had once visited and loved. Here, he stayed until the Chinese came.

For most of his later life Aufschnaiter continued to live in the Himalayan region, working as an agricultural engineer in Nepal. Every three years he visited his home in Austria and went mountaineering with his old friend, Harrer. Much later, he returned for good to Austria, where he lived until he passed away in 1973. His memoirs were published after his death in a book titled *Eight Years in Tibet*.

5 Coming of Age

When Kundun was around twelve, he lost the two most important figures in his life—his father Choekyong Tsering and his former Regent, Reting Rinpoche, the man who had recognized him as the Dalai Lama.

While Kundun's father died of illness, Reting Rinpoche's death was shrouded in controversy. Regency has for long been blamed for being the weak spot in Tibetan politics. The Regent is entrusted with the enormous task of running the country between the death of one Dalai Lama and the assumption of power by the next. Decades are spent under the rule of the Regent who, however, commands far less loyalty and affection from the people, unlike the Dalai Lamas who are seen as God-Kings. So too it was with Reting Rinpoche. His position as Regent was not without rumours of corruption and he was eventually forced to give up the Regency. His place was taken by Kundun's Junior Tutor, Taktra Rinpoche. In 1947, a civil war broke out between the followers of these two monks. Reting Rinpoche was arrested on charges of trying to assassinate Taktra Rinpoche and worse still, of conspiring with the Chinese. He died rather mysteriously in prison.

Following his arrest, Reting Rinpoche had sought

for a meeting with the young Kundun but the request had been denied. Kundun himself was kept out of the entire episode and he could only try and speculate on what was happening outside. Young though he was, he did realize that the Tibetan feudal system with the monks holding so much power was not good for the country. And the death of Reting Rinpoche genuinely saddened him.

This marked the beginning of change in Tibet.

Tibetan social system was what is called feudal theocracy. This means that the monasteries were powerful and owned much of the land on which people worked. The power lay with a few people only and the majority of the people were poor, overworked and underpaid. Over the years, people were beginning to tire of this, and the feudal system was already on shaky grounds by the time Reting Rinpoche died. Corruption was rampant in political circles and the Chinese began to take advantage of the vulnerable situation. In 1948, Chinese spies were reported in Tibet.

And then in 1950, when Kundun was barely sixteen, the People's Republic of China under Mao Tse Tung began her invasion of Tibet. There had been no prior warning. The Tibetan army was too small to tackle them. The brave Khampa (from the Kham region) warriors tried to hold the Chinese back unsuccessfully. News of this reached Lhasa where the Kashag or the cabinet was called. The Oracle was also summoned. In the Tibetan tradition, it is not at all uncommon to approach the Oracle for divine guidance. Here, a monk who can connect with the protector spirits is consulted and guidance is sought from the spirit. The Oracle becomes the vehicle through whom the protector deity communicates. It is an elaborate process and not to be taken lightly. The State Oracle is the Nechung Oracle through whom the protector deity called Dorje Drakden communicates.

The verdict was clear, 'His time has come'. Kundun was to assume power immediately and take over the responsibility of running the government. He was still two years short of attaining majority. Kundun himself also felt that he was too young to take on charge, but as he reveals in his autobiography, in this matter he was not consulted.

When the news spread that Kundun was going to take over his political duties, the people of Tibet were happy but the Chinese were not. Kundun's oldest brother, Thubten Jigme Norbu, the Abbot of Kumbum monastery, was among those who had to deal with the Communist firsthand. He was asked to persuade his brother, the Dalai Lama, to align with the Communist rule. And to his absolute horror, they suggested that he kill his brother if he opposed the Chinese. Thubten Jigme Norbu set out for Lhasa as directed. But once there, he warned Kundun about the troubles that were brewing and the severity of it. Further, he chose to renounce his monastic path. Thubten Jigme Norbu then prepared to leave for the United States to seek support for Tibet from the Americans.

In Lhasa, preparations for Kundun's coronation began and the date was fixed for 17 November 1950. On the morning of his coronation, Kundun's Master of Robes brought him his finest robes and a green sash to be tied at the waist, for luck.

The first order that Kundun gave on assuming temporal power was to release the prisoners. He had for long watched them through the telescope and considered them to be his friends. Later that day, when he went out on the terrace and looked through his telescope, he saw the empty prison yard. Not surprisingly, he missed the prisoners.

With Kundun's taking over as the political head of state, the Regent, Taktra Rinpoche, resigned from his post.

As the head of Tibet, Kundun made another wise decision—he appointed two Prime Ministers, Lobsang Tashi, a monk and Lukhangwa, a layman. Next, he sent appeals to the powerful countries in the west including the United States and Great Britain, and also to his neighbours, Nepal and China. His ministers also appealed to the United Nations:

'The problem is simple. The Chinese claim Tibet as a part of China. Tibetans feel that racially, culturally, and geographically they are far apart from the Chinese. If the Chinese find the reactions of the Tibetans to their unnatural claim not acceptable, there are other civilised methods by which they could ascertain the views of the people of Tibet; or, should the issue be surely juridical, they are open to seek redress in an international court of law. The conquest of Tibet by China will only enlarge the area of conflict and increase the threat to the independence and stability of other Asian countries. We Ministers, with the approval of His Holiness the Dalai Lama, entrust the problem of Tibet in this emergency to the ultimate decision of the United Nations, hoping that the conscience of the world will not allow the disruption of our State by methods reminiscent of the jungle.'

The Kashag (Cabinet) and National Assembly of Tibet, Kalimpong.

Britain, however, dismissed the issue of Tibet in the UN General Assembly. India too was of the opinion that talks between Tibet, China and India should be peaceful and sorted amongst the three countries. With that, the one beacon of hope that Tibet held from the world was lost.

Meanwhile at Tibet's eastern borders, the Chinese forces grew in numbers. There was no way that the Tibetan army could hold them off. The safety of the newly instituted head of Tibet was a big concern. The cabinet decided that he should shift to southern Tibet, to a place called Dromo, just short of the Sikkim border. Leaving his Prime Ministers in charge, Kundun left with his senior officials. Dromo was chosen for if circumstances proved necessary, Kundun could escape into India and seek asylum.

The Tibetans were not entirely unfamiliar with this state of affairs. The 13th Dalai Lama too had lived in exile, once in Mongolia in 1902 and again, in India for three years when the Chinese Manchu dynasty invaded Tibet in 1909.

Meanwhile, a delegation led by an official named Ngabo Ngawang Jigme made its way to Peking, as Beijing was then called, to enter into talks with the Communist government. They were to try and convince the Communist Party to withdraw their troops from Tibet.

Kundun waited for news of a possible negotiation. Imagine his horror when instead, the radio blared the news that Ngabo Ngawang Jigme had signed a Seventeen Point Agreement for 'a peaceful liberation of Tibet'. Kundun in his autobiography *My Land and My People* describes the moment: 'We first came to know of it from a broadcast which Ngabo made on Peking Radio. It was a terrible shock when we heard the terms of it. We were appalled at the mixture of Communist clichés, vainglorious assertions which were completely false, and bold statements which were only partly true and the terms were far worse and more oppressive than anything we had imagined.' Ngabo Ngawang Jigme later claimed that his delegation had been forced to sign the agreement which granted China sovereignty over Tibet.

In any case, Ngabo Ngawang Jigme did not return to Lhasa as a hero. And the consequences of his actions had only just begun.

In Dromo, news that the new Chinese General appointed for Tibet would arrive via India and therefore pass Dromo reached Kundun. A meeting was unavoidable. The General, a man named Chiang Chin Wu, carried a letter from Mao Tse Tung which repeated again that the Chinese were welcoming the Tibetans back to the 'great motherland', a phrase Kundun had begun to detest more and more.

With these developments, Kundun decided to go back to Lhasa. He had been away for nine months. The people were happy when their young ruler returned to his seat. In Lhasa, people brought stories of the unrest caused by the Chinese invasion, the atrocities perpetuated on the Tibetan people, and yet they were not willing to give up hope. Kundun listened to them all.

Back in his palace, he also met with tragic news—his favourite playmate, the sweeper Norbu Dhondup, had died while he had been away. Norbu had been a constant friend to Kundun right from the time he became the Dalai Lama. He had happily joined him in his pranks, in fighting mock battles and in cheering up the boy. With Norbu's death, Kundun felt that he had well and truly left his childhood behind. He was now a man, the leader of six million Tibetans, and he had to prepare for his meeting with the Chinese delegation.

The 13th Dalai Lama, Thupten Gyatso, was a man of foresight and a great political strategist. He ruled at the time when the British held power in a large part of southern Asia. He managed to establish cordial relations with the British. On the other side of the border, he worked to maintain relations with the Chinese. Even so, Tibet had been invaded by the Qing dynasty. The last testament of the Great Thirteenth from the year 1933 is uncannily prophetic.

> 'Remember I am now reaching my fifty-eighth year and as you all are aware that between me and the new reincarnation there will be a period when there will be no ruler. Take measures now . . . If you are not able to defend yourselves now, the institutions of the Dalai Lama, venerable incarnates and those who protect the Teachings shall be wiped out completely. Monasteries shall be looted, property confiscated and all living beings shall be destroyed . . . All souls shall be immersed in suffering and the night shall be long and dark.'

It is believed that Thupten Gyatso's death in 1933, at the age of fifty-eight, was preordained so that when trouble came to Tibet's doors, the next incarnation would be old enough to face it. And so it came to be.

Why did China want to invade Tibet?

Mary Craig in her book, *Kundun* cites 'land, mineral resources, strategic position and naked power' as the driving force. China's invasion of Tibet came soon after its invasion of East Turkestan (now called Xinjiang) and Taiwan. Having the roof of the world in her kitty would make China a country to contend with in all of Asia. The vast plains of Tibet offered more land to accommodate China's teeming population. Tibet's untapped mineral resources may have well been another reason. Furthermore, in today's water climate, Tibet as the source of the rivers Brahmaputra, the Yangtze, and the Mekong, among others, is of supreme economic importance to China.

6 The Dragon and the Elephant

A few years after the Chinese invasion, the Communist government issued an invitation to the Dalai Lama to visit China. Kundun accepted. He saw this as an opportunity to put forward his country's interests and speak directly to Chairman Mao Tse Tung, the head of the Communist Party which then ruled China.

Kundun set out for China in July 1954 with 500 officials accompanying him. The journey itself took two months and involved as many modes of transport as one can think of—travel by coracle, by the old Dodge that belonged to the 13th Dalai Lama, by mules where the road was under construction, by aircraft, train, jeep and even a truck!

Kundun's impressions of Peking, and indeed all of China, was that it bore an air of drab efficiency. Everyone was clad in grey suits and this was a stark contrast to the royal resplendence of the Tibetan officials who wore elaborate robes, headgear and jewellery. Communist China had lost its colour when it rejected all traditions and festivities, customs and rituals. Life had been trimmed to bare essentials and the changed attitude reflected in the clothes people had to wear and the lifestyles they led.

In Peking, Kundun met with Chairman Mao several times, and was deeply impressed by him. In the course of their discussions, which were almost always on Tibet, Mao said, 'Tibet is a great country. You have a marvellous history. Long ago, you even conquered a lot of China. But now you have fallen behind and we want to help you.' Kundun was overjoyed after these meetings. It seemed as if there was indeed ground for discussion. With genuine interest, Kundun used his time in China to study how Communism worked, and understand the progress that the Chinese had made. He agreed with much of the Marxist philosophy, and endorsed the idea of equality for all. So much so that Kundun considered becoming a member of the Communist Party.

Mao even went on to form a Preparatory Committee consisting mainly of Tibetans, and under the direct authority of Kundun, in order to 'prepare' Tibet to become a part of China. Kundun accepted it as a way of buying some time. He also welcomed ideas and suggestions from the Chinese about modernizing Tibet.

However, gradually in the long months that Kundun spent in China, his disillusionment with the system began to grow. He was not allowed to mingle with the local people. Under the guise of security, his meetings with foreign dignitaries were monitored by Chinese officials. Every move he made was recorded and reported to the authorities. He began to feel first-hand the stifling oppression of Communism.

It was also apparent that Mao and Communist China's atheism would never work in Tibet. During his last meeting with Kundun, before he left for Lhasa, Mao said to the young Tibetan leader 'Religion is poison.'

On his return journey, Kundun and his entourage stopped often at various settlements to meet the Tibetan people who flocked in large numbers at this rare honour of seeing their God–King. One such stop was at Taktser and Kumbum, Kundun's old home. Taktser being very close to the border had been one of the earliest villages to come under Chinese rule.

At Taktser, when Kundun asked the people if they were satisfied with the new regime, they replied, 'Yes, we are very happy under the Communist rule.' But as they said this, their eyes were filled and many could barely hold back their tears. Communist indoctrination had already begun. The Tibetan people living here were now forced into roadwork and farming. Their lives had changed overnight and they were, in reality, terribly unhappy.

And yet, the problem was not with the individual Chinese people. Indeed some of them had deep respect for the Dalai Lama. At one stop on this journey, a tough looking Chinese guard came up to the Kundun's jeep and asked, 'Where is the Dalai Lama?'

'Here,' said the Tibetan officials, pointing to Kundun. The guard at once took off his hat and approaching Kundun reverently, requested for a blessing.

The summer of 1955 was by far the most peaceful of the decade. But summer in Tibet, says Kundun, is a very short season. Sure enough, bad news was on its way. To say that the people were unhappy with the Chinese invasion is an understatement. From the borders, refugees started pouring into Lhasa with stories of oppression and torture, with news of unreasonable taxes, with horror reports of arrests and even of deaths. The rebellion from the people spilled into the streets of Lhasa where posters and songs demanded that the Chinese go back to their country.

A guerilla army was formed called the Khampa/Amdowa Freedom Fighters Alliance. The Chinese government demanded that the 'insurgents' be put down. The two Prime Ministers supported the people. Lukhangwa, especially, was very vocal in conveying his anger to the Chinese officials in Lhasa. Kundun continued to try to be the balance between the Chinese and the Tibetans, still believing that dialogue was possible and bloodshed could be avoided. As tensions rose and tempers wore thin, both the Prime Ministers chose to resign. Personally, Kundun realized for the first time what it meant to be a political head. He continued, however, his religious practice and often yearned to give up politics for a life devoted to spirituality alone.

The land of the Buddha . . .

It was the 2,500th Buddha Purnima celebrations in India and an invitation was extended to Kundun. Under the troubled circumstances, he was overjoyed. It meant, getting out of the complicated situation for at least a brief period, visiting the 'Aryabhumi' or the Buddha's land, stepping into the country of the Mahatma, and being given an opportunity to meet Prime Minister Nehru and seek his help.

Of course, the Chinese officials sent him off with detailed instructions on what he could say and what he couldn't. They even accompanied him to the Tibetan border. Once across the border, free of the overbearing Chinese supervision, Kundun felt liberated, excited and enthusiastic about his visit to India. He crossed into Sikkim where he was welcomed by the Maharaj Kumar of Sikkim, Thondup Namgyal. Sikkim was then an independent kingdom and had an Indian political officer stationed there. The Sikkimese prince greeted Kundun with a *khata* or a silk scarf, as is done in the Tibetan tradition, and a garland as is done in India. Kundun was flown to Delhi where the Prime Minister Jawaharlal Nehru and the Vice-President Rajendra Prasad waited to welcome him.

Later Kundun also met the President Dr Radhakrishnan and felt that in the Indian leaders, he was in the company of intellectuals—politicians he could bring himself to respect and trust.

One of the first things Kundun did in Delhi was to visit the Raj Ghat, to pay his respects to Mahatma Gandhi. Kundun had never met the Mahatma but had, like many other world leaders, followed his life with interest, and had tremendous respect for Gandhiji's path of non-violence. Standing there, Kundun felt a reaffirmation of his decision to abide by peace and non-violence. And this faith has remained with him throughout his life.

After the Buddha Jayanti celebrations, Kundun met Nehru. At this meeting, Kundun felt bold enough to express his true concerns about the Tibetan situation. India, under Nehru had signed a treaty with China called the Panch Sheel Agreement, a few years earlier. As a newly independent country, India was trying to establish cordial relations with her neighbours and the Panchsheel or Five Principles of Peaceful Coexistence stressed on mutual respect for each other and non-interference between the two countries. According to this agreement, India accepted that Tibet was a part of China. So now, Nehru listened to Kundun's concerns but conveyed India's stance of non-interference in the Tibet-China relationship. He further advised Kundun to try and work with the Seventeen Point Agreement and not to antagonize China.

It was a disappointed Kundun who continued on his pilgrimage. He visited Ajanta, Bodhgaya, Sarnath, Sanchi and Benares. What caught his attention was the sense of freedom in the country. He saw first-hand how democracy worked. For instance, Nehru did not agree with Kundun on several issues but not once was Kundun prevented from expressing his views. Likewise, there was no restriction on Kundun's movements and he travelled through the country freely. In the Buddhist towns, people thronged to see him and seek his blessings. And the lingering impression of India was that people were at liberty to lead their lives according to their will.

Kundun's pilgrimage was cut short by an urgent call from the Chinese Ambassador summoning him to Delhi. In the capital, Kundun met the Chinese Premier Chou En Lai who was then in India. Chou En Lai spoke agitatedly about the troubles in Lhasa, the threat of an uprising and the rumour that Kundun was planning to stay on in India.

This was not a far-fetched rumour. The Kundun was in fact, considering seeking asylum in India. His brothers, Thupten Jigme Norbu and Gyalo Dhondup were then in India and advised Kundun against going back to Tibet. They were confident of the United States' support for Tibet. Lukhangwa, Kundun's former Prime Minister, also made his way into India on the pretext of coming on pilgrimage. He too was of the opinion that it was not safe for Kundun to return. The situation in Tibet had worsened. Nehru, as expected, asked Kundun to return to Tibet. On his part he promised to speak to Chou En Lai.

Kundun sought the Oracle. The Oracle's advice was that Kundun must go back to Tibet. Lukhangwa tried to persuade him. 'When men become desperate they consult Gods,' he said. 'And when gods become desperate, they lie.'

Kundun understood his concern but decided to return to Tibet in March 1957. It had not been an easy decision to take, but he felt he must make one more attempt for peace.

On the journey home, Kundun saw the Tibetan

prayer flags flutter in the wind. Only, they were now outnumbered by the red flags of Communist China. And on entering Tibet, he immediately felt the sensation of oppression and a loss of freedom.

Communism and Democracy

China was a monarchy and from the 17th century had been ruled by the Manchu dynasty, which gradually weakened in power. In 1912, the Kuomintang party founded by Sun Yat Sen succeeded in overthrowing the monarchy and his socialist democratic party assumed power. Between 1937 and 1945, there was war between China and Japan. It was only because of the attack on Pearl Harbour did Japan's hold on China weaken. In 1949, Communist forces led by Mao Tse Tung took over, beginning a hugely significant era in 20th-century Chinese history.

Communism in theory is quite wonderful because it focuses on people sharing wealth as opposed to capitalism where only a few people profit. Pure Communism, as Karl Marx dreamt of, would result in an ideal society where people didn't need to be led. After years of monarchy and civil war, communism seemed to be the perfect answer to China's situation. But throughout the modern world, communism has never been a big success. In implementing a communist state, countries often actually ended up in establishing a dictatorial leadership. This in theory was to safeguard the idea of shared wealth while making sure that there is no rebellion from people. Marx thought that within a few generations, people would get used to living an equal life and the dictator would become redundant. It was a great dream but the dictatorial leadership proved to be disastrous. It gave one party enormous power and wealth. The people had no say in governance or economy. When they rebelled, they were oppressed. For the sake of an ideology, people ended up sacrificing personal freedom.

In contrast, democracy has proved to be a suitable form of governance. It's a government that rests all power in the hands of the people. Individual freedom is stressed as a fundamental right. In a democratic republic, people, rather than being directly involved in decision making, elect representatives who govern the country on their behalf. When India became independent of colonial rule in 1947, she chose to be a socialist democratic republic.

7 / Escape

Kundun was not merely the temporal head of Tibet but the spiritual head as well. He was a monk and the follower of a deeply spiritual path. This meant that he had to continue his studies through all the political upheaval that was taking place.

Kundun followed the Gelug-pa tradition of Tibetan Buddhism. There are four schools in Tibetan Buddhism and Gelug-pa is one of them. Here, monks take an exam to earn the *Geshe* degree. This is a bit like getting a PhD in the modern system of education. It usually takes around twenty years for a monk to prepare for this. For the final exam, the examinee has to participate in a debate in front of a huge audience of monks and teachers. Debating practice begins rather early in the monk's religious studies.

And so too it was for Kundun. That he was a Dalai Lama did not exempt him from exams and studies. Lessons progressed without a break.

It became increasingly apparent that the fate of Tibet was entwined with that of the Dalai Lama. He continued to be the pivot, balancing the Chinese government with the Tibetan government, and serving as the link between the Tibetan government and the

Tibetan people too! By now, there were thousands of refugees in Lhasa who had come from the borderlands of Tibet. Chinese atrocities against the people grew. Monasteries were plundered and villages were destroyed. People were left landless and homeless. The Khampa warriors went underground forming guerrilla bands and several people joined them. The Chinese administration demanded that the Tibetan government stop them. The Kashag was shocked—Tibetans to fight Tibetans?!

Kundun's final exams were scheduled for early March 1959 to coincide with the Monlam Festival. The exams and the festivities ran simultaneously for over a week. In the midst of the preparations, a couple of junior officials came to the Jokhang Temple, the venue for the programme. They informed the Kundun of a theatrical performance that was being planned by the Chinese and requested a confirmation of Kundun's participation and his preferred date.

Now, Kundun was right then preoccupied with the events that were already taking place. He offered to give them a date once the ceremonies ended in ten days time. A few days later, on 5th of March, the annual procession marking Kundun's return to the Norbulingka Palace took place. Curiously, this year, no Chinese officials were present at the event, unlike the previous years when they had actively participated in it.

Two days later, on the 7th, the Chinese officials called on Kundun's Chief Abbot, insisting on finalizing a date for the Kundun to watch the performance. Finally, the date was set to the 10th.

On the 9th of March, the Commander of Kundun's bodyguards, Kusung Depon, was summoned to the Chinese camp. He was to be briefed about the events of the following day. At the camp, Kusung Depon was shocked when he heard the directives: 'There will be none of the ceremony you usually have. None of your armed men are to come with him. No Tibetan soldier is to come beyond the Stone Bridge. If you insist he may have two or three Tibetan bodyguards, but it is definitely decided that none of them must be armed.'

The Stone Bridge marked the boundary of the Chinese camp in Lhasa. Kusung Depon returned to Norbulingka seething in anger. He had received no acceptable explanation from the Chinese general for these measures. It was very, very suspicious. Kundun however, decided to go ahead and attend the performance. His cabinet, the Kashag, would accompany him. It was also decided by the Tibetan officials that the Chinese demands would not be made public. The people were already so angry and so frustrated that only a small trigger was needed for things to spiral out of control.

However, news did get out and snowballed into the rumour that the Chinese planned to kidnap Kundun. People were agitated because at other instances, certain high officials had been invited by the Chinese for special events and had never been seen again. At this point there was open hostility between the Tibetans and Chinese.

That night Kundun slept restlessly. What would the next day bring? On the morning of the 10th, Kundun woke up at 5 a.m. and went to his prayer room. After his prayers, he stepped out into the garden. It was a beautiful spring morning. There was so much quiet and he felt at peace here. And these, he says, were the last moments of peace he was to know.

Outside, he heard shouts and sent his officials to find out what was happening. And as it turned out, the people of Lhasa as well as the refugees had decided to take matters into their hands and gathered together to protect their Kundun. Hundreds and thousands of people made their way to the Norbulingka and surrounded the palace. Their purpose was to prevent him from visiting the Chinese camp for the performance.

Lhasa was a city with a sizeable population, and now more crowded with the refugees. Moreover, they came in hordes to take their place beside their beloved Kundun. No one considered suspicious was allowed to enter the palace and this included quite a few Chinese drivers who had been assigned to some Tibetan officials. However riots soon began outside the Norbulingka in which one Tibetan official, who was considered too friendly with the Chinese, was killed.

Kundun heard the news with much sorrow. The leaders appointed by the people outside were called into the Norbulingka and informed that Kundun would not attend the theatrical performance. These leaders extracted a further promise from him that he would not attend any other events at the Chinese camp. With this guarantee, they agreed to withdraw. But several people stayed put outside the Norbulingka.

In the meantime, Kundun sent his officials to the

Chinese camp to inform General Tan Kuan-sen that he was not attending the programme. The Chinese General became very agitated and angry. He blamed the Tibetan government for doing nothing to suppress the 'reactionaries' and rather encouraging them in rebelling against the Chinese. Even as the Tibetans listened, perplexed, the officials proclaimed, 'This is rebellion. This is the breaking point. We shall act now, so be prepared.'

Kundun's men returned a worried lot. The people of Lhasa, meanwhile, grew bolder. Public meetings were held in all parts of the city and announcements were made by the leaders that Tibetans should rise and reject the Chinese rule. 'Tibet is for Tibetans' was the slogan of the day.

Inside the Norbulingka, a very worried Kundun and his officials discussed the situation. For the next two-three days, the tension remained. On the third day, a letter arrived from the Chinese General. Along with it came a letter from Ngabo Ngawang Jigme, the official who had signed the Seventeen Point Agreement. He wrote from the Chinese camp and accepted that there was no room for peace any more. He made another request, 'If Your Holiness with a few trusted officers of the bodyguard can stay within the inner wall, and hold position there, and inform General Tan Kuan-sen exactly which building you will occupy, they certainly intend that this building will not be damaged.'

It was now evident that the Chinese were planning an attack. Kundun tried buying time by writing to both

General Tan Kuan-sen and Ngabo. His worry was that the people surrounding Norbulingka were not safe and if an attack were to be launched, they were no match for the Chinese army.

Over the next few days, the inhabitants of Lhasa noticed weapons being brought into the Chinese camp at Lhasa and news reached Kundun of the impending attack. On the afternoon of the 16th, even as he sat discussing the next move with the Kashag, two mortar shells were fired from the Chinese camp. Outside, the people snapped! Inside the palace, Kundun and his Kashag sought the Oracle.

'Go,' he said. 'Go, tonight!'

It was a big decision. Kundun's life was not safe in Lhasa and yet was leaving the country the only way out? And what of his people? They were outside fighting for their Dalai Lama, fighting for Tibet. Could he just leave?

And yet, it was the best thing he could do. With Kundun in Lhasa, the battle was going to be too bloody. His people would not allow him to be captured and the Chinese were not going to give up. The fate of Tibet was so closely intertwined with Kundun's own that his safety meant that Tibet would still have some hope.

Those closest to him, the four members of the Kashag, his personal tutors and bodyguards, and members of his family who were still in Tibet—his mother and older sister and his youngest brother, Tenzin Choegyal, were to leave Lhasa with him. The Oracle had been most helpful this time by drawing the path they should take to India.

That night, Kundun went to offer prayers to his deity. He came out of the prayer room and took off his monk's robes. He would have to escape incognito. His disguise, ironically for a monk, was a soldier's uniform and cap. Wearing it, he came out of his chambers. A soldier held out a gun and Kundun took the weapon and slung it over his shoulder. At the gate Kusung Depon stood waiting. Kundun took off his glasses to complete his disguise and stepped out of the Norbulingka. Pretending to be guards on duty, they made their way through the crowds of people. No one stopped them. No one recognized them.

The Journey to India

If the Dalai Lama had maintained a brief journal of his flight it would perhaps have read something like this:

Day 1: Taking the south and south-east route to India. Crossed the river last night rather nervously. The oars were so loud that I was sure the Chinese soldiers would hear it. Knocked on a stranger's door at 3 a.m., looking for a place to rest.

Day 2: Left at dawn after thanking our hosts. I think they knew who I was but to their credit, said nothing. I wonder if news of my escape is out yet. We crossed our first mountain pass. On the way, an old man walked up to us and gifted me a white horse. It was good timing, our mules and ponies were already exhausted. Coming down the Che-La pass was easy.

It is very sandy and most of my group ran down happily. From the foot of the pass, we took a ferry across the Tsangpo River and reached Kyeshong (Happy) valley. Our first danger has been crossed.

Day 3: We are a group of 100 and it appears that the Tibetan soldiers and guerrillas have realized who we are and that we are escaping. There are a few hundred accompanying us, to protect us. We reach the village of Chenye. On radio The Voice of America reported violence in Lhasa. My whereabouts, it said, were unknown. So they know I have escaped.

Day 4: We are in the heart of the mountains. There is no turning back. Yet another pass to cross. Spending the night at a monastery. It's a good thing there are so many in Tibet!

Day 5: One more mountain pass. They are an ordeal and difficult to climb but at the top of the pass, there is often a beautiful sight. Today we arrived at a very fertile plateau. It was green and yaks grazed contentedly.

Day 6: A pass, a valley and a monastery for the night. We are meeting people who are giving us information about what happened in Lhasa after we left. It's very sad news. Norbulingka has been bombed. The rest of the city is also under attack and there are casualties. No one knows the exact number yet. Many buildings, houses, monasteries, even the medical college and parts of the Potala have been damaged, from what we hear.

Day 7: Reached the monastery at Lhuntze Dzong. From here, sent a messenger to ride before us to the Indian border, seeking asylum. Don't want to enter India without permission.

Everyone is weary and worried about what's happening in Lhasa.

Day 8: Continued on the journey. It is freezing. Hands and fingers are numb. The men who have moustaches have icicles on them. Another mountain pass. Reached Jhora village.

Day 9: Left Jhora at 4 in the morning. As we reached the top of a pass, we overheard an aircraft above us. There was nowhere to hide and we were a group of a few hundred people. Was it a Chinese aircraft? I don't know, but whoever it was could not have missed us! Everyone's uneasy.

Day 10: Still uneasy. Still plodding through the mountains.

Day 11: Nothing to report. Everyone is exhausted.

Day 12: Arrive in Mangmang, the last Tibetan settlement before the Indian border. Our messenger is back with news that the Indian government has granted me asylum. What a relief! It rained and I slept in a tent that leaked.

Day 13: Woke up with a fever. Still in Mangmang. The radio is on and I heard news about myself. Apparently I have fallen off a horse and am injured. I laughed when I heard it for that is perhaps the one misfortune I have managed to avoid so far.

We are one day away from the border. Our group is still a few hundred strong. We have to decide who would cross the border and who will not. The monks and officials would come with me while the soldiers and the guerrilla fighters close to remain in Tibet. I am moved by the loyalty and patriotism of my countrymen.

Day 14: Still have a fever but I ride the dzo across the border. We are safe.

It took the group a week and some more mountain passes to cross before they came to a village. They were

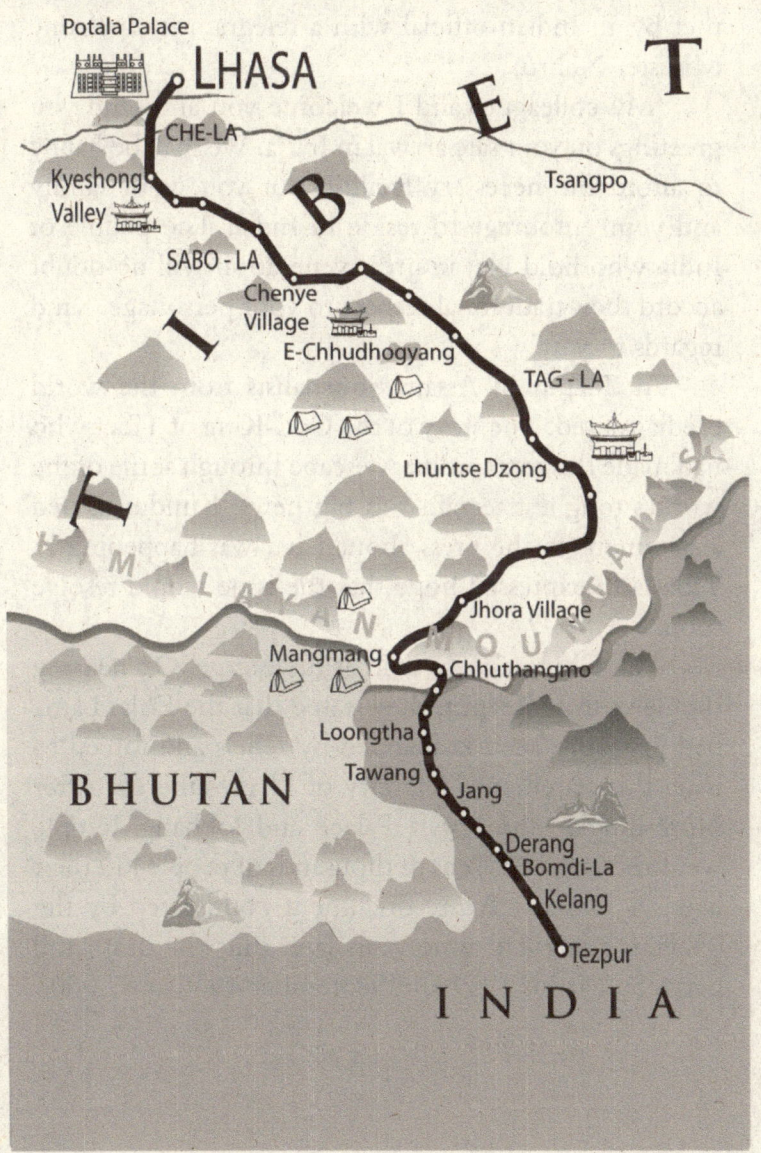

Potala Palace

LHASA

CHE-LA

Kyeshong Valley

SABO - LA

Chenye Village

E-Chhudhogyang

TAG - LA

Lhuntse Dzong

Tsangpo

TIBET

HIMALAYAN MOUNTAINS

Jhora Village

Mangmang

Chhuthangmo

Loongtha

Tawang

Jang

Derang

Bomdi-La

Kelang

Tezpur

BHUTAN

INDIA

met by an Indian official with a telegram from Prime Minister Nehru:

'My colleagues and I welcome you and send you greetings on your safe arrival in India. We shall be happy to afford the necessary facilities for you, your family and your entourage to reside in India. The people of India who hold you in great veneration will no doubt accord their traditional respect to your personage. Kind regards to you.'

At Tezpur in Assam, journalists from the world media waited. The story of the God-King of Tibet who had made this extraordinary escape through some of the world's toughest terrain was big news. Kundun issued a statement to the press about what was happening in Tibet and expressed hope that the issue would resolve soon.

The Chinese were livid at the escape. On hearing the news from Tezpur, they stated that the Dalai Lama had probably been kidnapped by rebels and forced to issue this statement. The city of Lhasa suffered. After Norbulingka, the Potala Palace and Jokhang Temple were also targeted. Tens of thousands of people lost their lives. A Chinese Army document confiscated by the Tibetan guerrillas some years later puts the death toll between March 1959 and September 1960 at 87,000.

The four schools of Tibetan Buddhism

There are four schools of Tibetan Buddhism—Nyingma, Kagyu, Sakya and Gelug. The fundamental philosophy is the same but the teachings and the path of monastic learning varies with each of them. The Nyingma is the oldest of the four. The Dalai Lama belongs to the Gelug school to which also belong the great monasteries of Sera, Drepung and Ganden. Gelug monks study for almost twenty years before they can hope to attain the highest rank of *Geshe*.

8 Beginning Exile

Making his way on the back of a white horse, Pandit Nehru reached Birla House in Mussorie where Kundun was staying. 'How are you doing?' asked the Indian Prime Minister.

Answered the Dalai Lama in his best English, 'I'm quite nice.'

For the first year after arriving in India, Mussoorie was Kundun's home. He began his exile by extensively discussing the events in Tibet with Prime Minister Nehru and with the International Commission of Jurists, a legal body that focuses on human rights. The issue, however, could not be taken to the United Nations as neither Tibet nor China were members of the UN at that time.

By 1960, the Indian government gave Kundun a permanent place to stay: it was a small bungalow called Swarg Ashram in the hill station of Dharamsala, in Himachal Pradesh. When Kundun and his entourage arrived at Dharamsala, it was rather late in the day. In the morning when he awoke, the view from his window was a vision to behold—the Himalayas—home.

Kundun's home was now shared by his mother and a few other members of his entourage. Dharamsala was going to be their residence for quite some time, of this there was no doubt. One of the first things Kundun did was start a nursery for the Tibetan refugee children. His older sister Tsering Dolma was put in charge of it.

While in Mussoorie, Kundun had already begun the process of change. Gone was the formality of Tibet where he was inaccessible to people. In exile, everyone was granted admission to see him. His new home was hardly the Potala. And Kundun did not complain.

The more immediate problem was the settlement of the refugees who continue to follow Kundun into exile. They came in large groups—peasants, nomads, merchants and monks. Sometimes entire families managed to escape but equally, many families were broken or separated in trying to escape. The refugees came into India and into Bhutan, all carrying horror stories of the invasion and attacks. Their escape was often as dramatic as Kundun's had been. Their arrival, though, was not. For many, the shock of the temperature in the plains of India brought on unheard of diseases. Several people died.

By 1960, there were several thousand Tibetan refugees in India. The Indian government found some work for them—road construction in Manali in the state of Himachal Pradesh. The refugees were hired as coolies. For most, the weather coupled with the extremes of hard labour proved unbearable. Kundun visited them and it was obvious that this was not a viable option. In the meantime, Nehru requested the state governments to consider rehabilitating the Tibetan refugees. Among the first to take the initiative was the Karnataka government which offered land in a place called Bylakuppe near Coorg. Only the most able-bodied of the refugees who could perhaps be able to withstand the weather were sent here.

The refugees from Tibet, still unaccustomed to the weather in India, did not immediately take to Bylakuppe. But they knew, as well as everyone did, that there were few other options available. The most difficult thing in resettling for them was to clear the forest area to begin their own lives. Tibetan Buddhists consider the karmic effects of all their actions very seriously. According to their belief, karma is the result of one's actions; if you do good, your karma is automatically good and vice versa. Taking another living being's life knowingly is an absolute horror and, very bad karma. Many Tibetans suffered deeply when they cut down trees and cleared the ground soil for agriculture.

During the first half of the 1960s, other Indian states too opened their doors to the Tibetan refugees and around twenty settlements came up across the country. Some were agricultural in nature while in some others, the main occupation was making handicrafts. Both kinds of livelihood posed several challenges but they were infinitely better than road construction. And so the rehabilitation process began.

Of utmost importance within these settlements was to preserve the Tibetan culture, language and religion, all of which had been in danger of being overpowered by Communist rule inside Tibet. Schools for children were set up, the Library of Tibetan Works and Archives was established in Dharamsala, and construction of monasteries, of such great importance to the Tibetan people, was also started.

Kundun's religious education and practice too resumed. As much as possible, the old ways of life from Tibet continued in exile but definitely with far less pomp and grandeur.

India's wars

China, in the meantime, did not react well to the Indian support of Kundun or the Tibetan people. Only recently had China and India established a rapport. 'Hindi Cheeni Bhai-Bhai' was the mood and the slogan. On 20 October 1962, Chinese forces entered Indian territory across the border, into Ladakh and Assam. Their claim was that India had encroached beyond the territory allowed to her, the McMahon Line,* as decided in 1953. Indian forces were not prepared for this invasion and lost the war, which ended with a Chinese ceasefire in November. It was a short battle but both sides had casualties. A deeper damage was that done to the relationship between the two Asian giants.

Kundun watched the happenings with anxiety and uneasiness. India and China had never shared a border before. Tibet had always buffered the two countries and

---

* The McMohan Line was agreed upon by Great Britain and Tibet as the boundary between China and India. It is named after Sir Henry McMohan, the foreign secretary of British India who negotiated the agreement in 1912.

now things had changed. Nehru took things to heart. In 1964, he breathed his last. Some historians believe that Nehru's death was a result of his shock at the Indo-China war. Lal Bahadur Shastri took over the reins as Prime Minister of India. During his leadership, India and her other neighbour Pakistan were at war with each other again over differences on the border issue. This war lasted longer than the war with China. India won the combat but soon after, Lal Bahadur Shastri too passed away. In the year 1966 Nehru's daughter Indira Priyadarshini was sworn in as Prime Minister.

In 1971, once more India and Pakistan were at war, this time over East Pakistan. India helped the region known as East Pakistan gain independence. It was renamed Bangladesh. This war also saw a new inclusion in the Indian army—Section 22—the regiment consisting of Tibetan refugees.

Section 22 was formed after the 1962 war, beginning with the Khampa guerrillas of Tibet. Eventually 12,000 men, mostly Khampas, became part of this Special Frontier Force, to be trained and sent into Tibet, in the event of another war with China. That, however, did not happen. But when India went to war with Pakistan in 1971, Prime Minister Indira Gandhi sent a message to the Tibetan regiment. She sought the help of the regiment in India's war against Pakistan. The Tibetans readily agreed to fight. Many saw it as a way of repaying India's generosity and hospitality. In this war there were casualties in this division but unfortunately, they have never been publicly acknowledged by India.

Eventually, several fighters from this regiment retired from the army and were rehabilitated in a settlement in Orissa.

The Cultural Revolution in China

Even as the Tibetan refugees struggled to regain their footing in an alien environment, China and, therefore, Tibet were going through a dark period—the Cultural Revolution. For the decade from 1966 to 1976, until Chairman Mao died, China went through one of her worst years. The Cultural Revolution was part of Mao's attempt to create a 'new' China. And in doing so, his civilian army known as the Red Guards wrecked havoc. 'Old ideas, old customs, old culture, old habits' were to be removed from the society in the name of revolution.

Before this, China had a rich tradition of rituals, beliefs and art. For religion, most people followed Confucianism, a philosophical system based on the teachings of the great thinker Confucius. All of this was suppressed and methodically destroyed during the Cultural Revolution. There was no freedom for the people. The education system suffered as the only teaching that took place was Communist propaganda. Intellectuals were not allowed to voice their views. In trying to create a society of equals, this period destroyed the wealth of free thought and speech. Those who tried to dissent were imprisoned, put to death or else sent for 're-education' in Maoist thought. Much of history was lost.

In Tibet, the Cultural Revolution made things worse than they already were with the invasion. Here, severe religious persecution took place. Several monasteries were destroyed. Some estimate the number at 6,000. Among the population, monks and nuns were targeted along with rich landlords and wealthy peasants. They were publicly humiliated by the Red Guards and the death toll went up. Imagine being told that you cannot wear your hair in the traditional way, or pray in a temple or turn the prayer wheel if you wanted to. The rules also meant that one could not sing traditional songs or perform customary dances. Further, in an effort to create a new generation of Communists, children were separated from their parents and sent away to study in Communist schools.

In India, no news reached Kundun from within Tibet. It was as if China and the regions she had invaded had closed themselves to the world. The only news came from people who lived in the border areas of India and Nepal and bartered with those within the Tibetan borders. Through their interaction some news was shared. And whatever little information came, it was not at all pleasant or encouraging. The Cultural Revolution had also put on hold any chance of the Tibetans returning home. It was clear to Kundun and the Kashag that the exile was not going to end anytime soon.

Even so, the death of Chairman Mao in 1976 brought some hope. The Chinese themselves were not prepared to accept the consequences of the Cultural Revolution. Hua Guofeng succeeded Mao as the Chairman and it was he who put an end to the Cultural Revolution. He was soon replaced by Deng Xiaoping, who seemed to be a liberal and promising leader.

Deng's emissaries got in touch with Gyalo Dhondup, Kundun's brother. They wanted to meet and open the lines of communication between their government and Kundun. As it is, the Chinese government was asking the Tibetans to return to Tibet.

It seemed opportune then that Kundun send a delegation to Tibet, to meet the new government and also see for themselves how things had been in the two decades they had been away. On 2 August 1979, a Tibetan delegation from Dharamsala left for Peking. Between August and October, they travelled through Tibet to see if the progress the Chinese bragged about could be true. They returned to Dharamsala with little positive news. The damage done by the years before and during the Cultural Revolution was very apparent. What's more the people of Tibet still yearned for their Kundun. The Communist propaganda amongst the people was not successful because despite the fact that their religion and culture was suppressed, the Tibetans held on to it in their hearts. They earnestly wanted freedom and independence, and life as they had known before the invasion.

The delegation came back with 7,000 letters, the first time any mail was exchanged between the people within Tibet and their families in exile.

Settlements in exile

There are approximately 1,00,000 Tibetans in India, followed by 16,000 in Nepal, Bhutan with 1883 and 25,712 across the world, mostly Switzerland, Canada, USA and Australia. In India, there are presently thirty-nine settlements, of which fourteen are in Himachal Pradesh, five in Karnataka, and the others in Jammu and Kashmir, Orissa, West Bengal, Sikkim, Arunachal Pradesh, Uttaranchal, Chhattisgarh, Meghalaya, Maharashtra, and Delhi.

The settlements in India are rather special because they allow the Tibetans the freedom to retain their own culture, language and tradition, without necessitating their assimilation into Indian society. Almost every settlement has a monastery, a Tibetan medical centre called the Men Tsee Khang, a school that follows the CBSE syllabus but includes Tibetan as a language, as well as little restaurants and cafés where Tibetan food is cooked and sold. In the settlements, people, especially the women, always wear their traditional dress, the *chuba*. Men may wear it on special occasions.

The settlements are agriculture or industry-based. Carpet weaving and handicrafts form the bulk of the industry. Many Tibetans travel all over the country in the winter months in order to sell sweaters. For several Tibetans, this is the only time they venture out of the settlement. The younger generation of Tibetans, however, are today stepping out of the settlements to study in colleges and to find employment in cities.

9 A New Era, or So It Seemed

In exile, Kundun was still the spiritual and temporal head of Tibet, now an occupied country. He still had to think about what had to be done next towards securing independence for his country and her people. In 1967, he began reaching out to the rest of the world. Although most invitations came to him as a Buddhist leader and a revered monk, Kundun also used these sojourns abroad to build awareness about the Tibetan issue. In 1967, he visited Japan and Thailand. A few years later, in 1973, he went to Europe. This was the beginning of a close relationship between Kundun and the West. On this trip, he also met his old friend Heinrich Harrer. Kundun also travelled to Switzerland, which was one of the first countries apart from India to open her doors to Tibetan refugees. Two hundred children had been adopted into Swiss families. Kundun visited them. In 1979, he went on a trip to the USSR, Mongolia and the United States of America.

The world, especially the United States and Europe, gradually began to understand what Kundun and the Tibetan people were talking about. The Chinese Cultural Revolution and its aftermath revealed the truth behind the Tibetans' stories. Kundun also gained support among the locals, intellectuals and even travellers to Tibet. When China in her post-Cultural Revolution mood opened her doors to travellers, journalists and other media, many people made their way into Tibet to see how things were after all these years of occupation.

From among the Tibetans in exile, two fact-finding missions went to Tibet. The first one comprised young people who only had a brief sojourn in Tibet while the second, and more successful one, was made up of educators, led by Kundun's younger sister Jetsun Pema. Between the travellers' reports and those of his own fact-finding missions, it was obvious to Kundun that things were not going so well within Tibet. Yet another delegation consisting of senior members of the cabinet visited Peking, this time to negotiate with the Chinese. This team held the view that Tibetans were a separate race and the Seventeen Point Agreement was not valid as the Tibetans did not accept it. With this intention, was there any possibility for negotiation?

The Chinese in turn wanted Kundun to return to Tibet, guaranteeing him the position he had held before 1959. They, however, refused to accept the Tibetan viewpoint, instead asking Kundun and the Tibetans to work for unity with China. Again, the two parties had arrived at a dead end.

Despite this, Kundun wanted to stay committed to the path of non-violence in seeking Tibet's freedom. He refused to think of waging a battle or fighting a war.

In *Freedom in Exile,* he writes:

'In the past, the idea of non-violent revolution had seemed perhaps idealistic, and I drew comfort from this overwhelming proof to the contrary. Chairman Mao once said that political power comes from the barrel of a gun. He was only partly right ... In the end, people's love for truth, justice, freedom and democracy will triumph. No matter what governments do, the human spirit will always prevail.'

Mahatma Gandhi was one of Kundun's biggest inspirations. His path of non-violence in the Indian independence movement left a profound impact on Kundun. As a Buddhist, he deeply abhorred violence. And there was already so much of it within Tibet following the Chinese invasion. With this in mind, he proposed a Five-Point Peace Plan for Tibet at the Human Rights Caucus in Washington, United States in 1987. Accordingly, he sought:

- The transformation of the whole of Tibet into a zone of peace.
- Abandonment of China's population transfer policy, which threatens the very existence of the Tibetans as a people. Due to China's population woes, many Chinese are sent to live in Tibet, and in Lhasa, it is said that the Chinese now outnumber Tibetans.
- Respect for the Tibetan people's fundamental human rights and democratic freedom.
- Restoration and protection of Tibet's natural environment and the abandonment of China's use

of Tibet for the production of nuclear weapons and dumping of nuclear waste.

- Commencement of earnest negotiations on the future status of Tibet and of relations between Tibetan and Chinese people.

Kundun envisioned Tibet as being a 'zone of ahimsa', the buffer between India and China. Here, he said, there will be no guns, no warfare and no bloodshed. Here, people, animals and indeed the entire ecosystem will remain protected from damage. The focus will be on peace and human rights.

The Five-Point Peace Plan was a wonderful idea but did not find any takers among the Communist Chinese. They accused Kundun of trying to create a split among the people of China, in which they included the Tibetan people.

Meanwhile, in Lhasa, people followed the developments with alternating hope and disappointment. Despite Communist efforts to indoctrinate the people and turn them against the Dalai Lama, the Tibetan people had remained loyal to Kundun. And as long as Kundun and the Kashag were present, the Tibetan people looked to them as the only valid government for Tibet. When news reached that Kundun's proposals had not been accepted by the Chinese, anger and resentment began to build up in Lhasa.

Between October 1987 and May 1990 several protests and demonstrations took place in Lhasa and other parts of Tibet. On 1 October 1987, some monks outside the Jokhang Temple in Lhasa raised the freedom call—*Bo*

Rangzen! [Freedom for Tibet!] Within minutes thousands of people had responded and began to gather outside the temple. For thirty long years, they had been subjected to oppression by the Communists and now they all rose in revolt. The Chinese were not prepared for this turn of events and began forcefully putting down the protestors. There were casualties on both sides. What was different this time, compared to what happened in 1959, was the presence of tourists and the western media. China had opened her doors to showcase the fact that the Cultural Revolution was truly over and so journalists were then present in Lhasa. And they now reported the incidents, which the rest of the world saw for the first time. So far, the world had only heard second-hand accounts about the Tibetan situation and could choose to believe either Kundun and the Government-in-exile or the Chinese regime. But now, the reality of the invasion of Tibet and the unhappiness of her people was there for all to see. Several protestors were immediately arrested and the world media was asked to leave Lhasa.

China blamed Kundun for instigating the people to revolt. He retorted, 'I am glad that the Chinese government have found in me a scapegoat for the Tibetan people's demonstrations in Tibet, just as they blamed the "Gang of Four"* for the madness and chaos of the

---

* The Gang of Four refers to four Chinese Communist officials, Mao's wife, Jiang Qing, Zhang Chunqiao, Yao Wenyuan, and Wang Hongwen. In the latter stages of the Cultural Revolution, they carried out several atrocities. They were later blamed for the worst of the Cultural Revolution and brought down from power a month after Mao's death.

Cultural Revolution. I appeal to all human rights groups to prevail upon the Chinese government to stop the executions and to release those imprisoned.'

Gyalo Dhondup, Kundun's brother, became the mediator between the Tibetan Kashag and the Chinese government. Messages went back and forth. On 10 March 1988, by now marked as the National Uprising Day in remembrance of the rebellion of 1959, Kundun issued a statement. He said, 'I have always felt that violence breeds violence. It contributes little to the resolution of conflicts. I, therefore, renew my appeal to all freedom-loving peoples to support our non-violent struggle for the survival of our national identity, our culture and our spiritual traditions, and to persuade the Chinese government to abandon its oppressive policies.'

The Chinese response was predictable; they said that they would negotiate only if Kundun gave up his demand for the independence of Tibet.

In June 1988, Kundun was invited to speak before the European parliament in Strasbourg, France. Addressing the parliament, he raised the issue of Tibet's independence. Before this audience he proposed the idea of 'genuine autonomy' for Tibet:

> 'The whole of Tibet known as Cholka-Sum
> (U-Tsang, Kham and Amdo) should become
> a self-governing democratic political entity
> founded on law by agreement of the people
> for the common good and the protection of
> themselves and their environment, in association

with the People's Republic of China. The Government of the People's Republic of China could remain responsible for Tibet's foreign policy. The Government of Tibet should, however, develop and maintain relations, through its own foreign affairs bureau, in the field of commerce, education, culture, religion, tourism, science, sports and other non-political activities.'

In response, the Chinese government asked him to come to Beijing for talks. Kundun preferred a more neutral ground like Geneva, but China refused. Again, it was a dead end.

But this was a decade of upheavals and incidents. In 1989, the 10th Panchen Lama, second only to the Dalai Lama in importance, died unexpectedly in Tibet. Now, traditionally, the Panchen Lama is not involved in the governance of the country. But his is an extremely high rank and the Panchen Lama is involved in the search for the Dalai Lama's incarnation and vice versa.

The Chinese had been for some time playing the Panchen Lama against the Dalai Lama. For a while the Panchen Lama had supported Communist China but when Dalai Lama went into exile, he began to speak up for the Tibetan people. The Panchen Lama was essentially a patriotic Tibetan. So when he died suddenly, and reportedly of heart attack, people suspected foul play. There were demonstrations in Lhasa. The Chinese declared a state of Emergency. Foreign media were not allowed to remain and martial law was declared. It looked like 1959 all over again.

The turning point was the student revolts in Beijing's Tiananmen Square. It seems the Tibetan people were not the only ones unhappy at the state of affairs. In the rest of China, the Cultural Revolution and its aftermath had created much unhappiness amongst the people.

In April 1989, Hu Yaobeng, a Party official, died and several thousand people gathered at his funeral. Among them were scores of students, for Hu Yaobeng had been known as a good reformer. The students demanded democratic reforms, and expressed dissent against the Communist authority. The protests grew in momentum and became a full-fledged demonstration. On 4th June, the Communist Army sent tanks to Tiananmen Square and opened fire! In this shocking incident, several civilians lost their lives.

The Western world condemned China while protests in Tibet continued as before. In all, between September 1987 and May 1990, there were around eighty demonstrations across Tibet, some small and others large. The protestors were killed, arrested, tortured and there was blatant abuse of human rights. Several political prisoners, who managed to escape, eventually made their way into India. Interestingly, oftentimes, it was monks who led the protests. As they continue to do even today.

Kundun was miserable, listening to the news. For all his desire for non-violence, it seemed to be a never-ending bloodbath. He says he admired his countrymen for their courage, but he also knew that violence was not going to solve the problem. He stuck to the path of ahimsa with great resolution. On all his travels, Buddhist teachings and the practice of ahimsa has been central to his discourses. The issue of Tibet is unavoidable but he also stresses on the oneness of humanity.

It is no surprise then that in 1989, the Nobel Committee named Kundun as the recipient of the Nobel Peace Prize, an award he accepted on behalf of the people of Tibet. In his Nobel acceptance speech in December 1989, he said:

I accept the prize with profound gratitude on behalf of the oppressed everywhere and for all those who struggle for freedom and work for world peace. I accept it as a tribute to the man who founded the modern tradition of nonviolent action for change—Mahatma Gandhi—whose life taught and inspired me. And, of course, I accept it on behalf of the six million Tibetan people, my brave countrymen and women inside Tibet, who have suffered and continue to suffer so much. They confront a calculated and systematic strategy aimed at the destruction of their national and cultural identities. The prize reaffirms our conviction that with truth, courage and determination as our weapons, Tibet will be liberated.

The 10th Panchen Lama

The Panchen Lama is considered the reincarnation of the Buddha Amitabha. Panchen Lama, meaning Great Scholar, was the title given by the 5th Dalai Lama, Ngawang Lobsang Gyatso, to his teacher, Lobsang Choekyi Gyaltsen. Consequently, the three incarnations before him came to be known as the 1st, 2nd and 3rd Panchen Lamas. Their seat is the Tashi Lhunpo monastery in the Tibetan city of Shigatse.

The relationship between the Dalai Lama and Panchen Lama has been of pupil and mentor, a bond built in trust, respect and affection. Each is involved in the selection and confirmation of the other's reincarnation.

The 10th Panchen Lama is perhaps the most controversial figure in Tibetan politics of the 20th century. Born Gonpo Tseten, the boy recognized as the 10th Panchen Lama was renamed Lobsang Trinley Lhundrub Choekyi Gyaltsen. This was during the reign of the Fourteenth Dalai Lama, in 1938. However, all was not smooth sailing during the time of the 10th Panchen Lama. Finding himself at loggerheads with the government in Lhasa, the Panchen Lama's association with the Chinese intensified. He began to openly express the view that Tibet should be considered a part of China.

The Communist Chinese took the Panchen Lama under their wing. They encouraged the rift between the Panchen Lama and the Dalai Lama, Tibet's two most important leaders. Choekyi Gyaltsen was only a few years younger than Kundun, and on occasions when the two met, there was no personal animosity between them. The two young men in fact took to each other, and their relationship was quite amicable. In fact, the Panchen Lama accompanied Kundun on his trips to both China and India.

When Kundun came into exile, he wrote to the Panchen Lama informing him of his decision. The Panchen Lama was brought to Lhasa on Kundun's exile. In 1962, the Panchen Lama gave a detailed report to the Chinese government criticizing the developments in Tibet post the Chinese occupation. He was promptly removed from his official duties, and arrested two years later. During the Cultural Revolution, he suffered greatly. He was imprisoned for almost a decade and even after his release, the Communist army ensured that he was kept under house arrest under their watchful vigilance in Beijing.

Choekyi Gyaltsen later gave up his vows as a monk and went on to marry and have a daughter. But for the people of Tibet, he was still the Panchen Lama and they were loyal to him. Some years later, in 1989, Choekyi Gyaltsen returned to his monastery, Tashi Lhunpo in Shigatse, and while here, he died unexpectedly. Many suspect that he was murdered for being a a patriot. Despite years of Communist indoctrination from the Chinese, and efforts to bring about discord between him and Kundun, the Panchen Lama remained a true Tibetan, loyal to his country and deeply respectful to the Dalai Lama.

10   Tibet? Dalai Lama!

Mention Tibet, and often the response it elicits is 'Dalai Lama'! For most of the world, Tibet has, over the years, become synonymous with the Dalai Lama. Kundun's teachings, and his chosen path of non-violence, have found wide appeal. He is often called the 'Gandhi of our times', reminding people that despite being a tough road to take, non-violence is definitely a better option.

    Kundun has become the face of Tibet, the man who put Tibet on the map, and made people aware that there was something terribly wrong going on here. On his travels, he says, he has a three-fold agenda—foremost as a human being who believes we all have a universal responsibility towards each other and towards nature, secondly as a Buddhist monk who seeks to create 'harmony and understanding between different religions', and thirdly, as a Tibetan and the Dalai Lama to speak about his country, her people and culture. His idea of Universal Responsibility has taken root in the establishment of the Foundation for Universal Responsibility of H.H. the Dalai Lama, set up with a portion of the Nobel Peace Prize money, an organization which has a global reach and aims to bring together people of different faiths, professions and nationalities.

Buddhism itself has grown in popularity in the last few decades, perhaps in the aftermath of the wars that shook so much of the early 20th century. One consequence of it is that Tibetan Buddhism and Kundun now have some high profile followers, all lending their voice and support to the cause of Tibet's freedom.

Kundun's appeal lies in the fact that despite the issue of Tibet's freedom, despite the rigours of exiled life, he has continued to be a practitioner of Buddhism. He insists that he is a 'simple Tibetan monk' first and foremost. His routine remains as stringent as it was in his childhood, and as dedicated to spiritual practice too. He has remained an early riser, waking up at 3.30 a.m. The next hour and a half, he spends in meditation and prayer. After a short walk, he has breakfast. As it was in the past, his breakfast continues to be a bowl of *tsampa* but with the addition of bread and porridge. Meditations and study of Buddhist scriptures continue until lunch is served at 11:30. Post lunch, Kundun visits his office. Interviews are often scheduled for this time. In the hours between tea and dinner, he returns to his prayers and meditation.

Kundun is not a vegetarian. One may argue that it seems hypocritical for a Tibetan Buddhist to talk about protecting life, while also eating meat. However, there is a reasoning for this. In Tibet's high altitude climate, very little vegetation grows and the people rely on meat for sustenance. It is unavoidable and indeed essential for survival. Having said that, in Tibet, rarely was a Buddhist seen among butchers.

Kundun says in his autobiography that he tried to give up eating meat after he came into exile. For two years he took to a vegetarian diet before contracting jaundice. On the doctor's advice, he resumed eating meat again. Nowadays, he limits his intake of meat. His kitchen in Dharamsala continues to serve only vegetarian food, as do the monastery kitchens in the various Tibetan settlements.

Criticism of Kundun's choices

It cannot be said that there has been no criticism of Kundun. In 1988, he addressed the European Parliament in Strasbourg, France. In his speech, Kundun shifted his stand from seeking complete independence to offering genuine autonomy as the solution for Tibet. This was called the Middle Way approach and it came under severe criticism from sections of the Tibetan population. Not everyone believed that it was the best approach for the Tibetan issue. Indeed, many felt it was an excuse for doing nothing about the situation. One of the groups to collectively voice this feeling was the Tibetan Youth Congress formed in 1970 by a small group of educated Tibetans. Their demand has been and remains that of complete independence for Tibet.

Kundun welcomed the criticism as someone who believes in democracy and the freedom of speech and opinion that it proffers. He had already started the process of democratizing his administration and in 2001, for the very first time, democratic elections for the post of Kalon Tripa or Prime Minister was held. Thus far, the Kalon Tripa was usually from a Tibetan noble family. Prof. Samdhong Rinpoche, a scholar and a senior monk, became the Kalon Tripa elected by the people. For the next term also, he found himself re-elected by the people with a massive majority of over 90 per cent of votes.

And then, China became the host country for the 2009 Olympics. On this occasion the Tibetan people decided to draw world attention to the issue of their occupied homeland again. In March 2008, trouble erupted in Lhasa. People took to the streets demanding independence. The protests, once again, were crushed using force. Tibetans in exile watched angry and helpless as news came from Lhasa. With the availability of cell phones and the Internet, everyone could access information readily and immediately. Tibetans on both sides were united with this power of connectivity.

In exile, weeks short of the Beijing Olympics, hundreds of Tibetans set out on a march towards Tibet, from Dharamsala. It was called the Tibetan People's Uprising Movement and they were taking a non-violent approach in their demand for independence. They also called for a boycott of the Games in China. Kundun asked them not to carry out this march, as it would offend the Indian government. He also refused to call for a boycott of the Beijing Games. For 103 days the group marched until they reached the Tibetan border on 19 June. Here they were arrested by the Indian police and thus prevented from continuing further on to Tibet.

In April of the same year, the Olympic torch made its way around the world. In several cities, including San Francisco, London and Paris, people expressed solidarity to the Tibetan cause by holding protests and peace marches. When the Olympic torch was about to enter India, over a hundred people were arrested to prevent them from causing trouble. What was to be a hugely celebrated event was reduced to a small occasion with low public attendance. With security personnel outnumbering the audience, mostly school children, the torch relay lasted a mere 2.3 km.

Tibet and Kundun were on the front page of magazines, in news channels and in cyber space. People were indeed listening.

Kundun, was again, accused by the Chinese of instigating these protests. Tired of denying these baseless accusations, and empathizing deeply with the growing frustration of his own people, Kundun did the most democratic thing a leader could—he asked the Tibetan people to decide what they wanted as the way forward. In November 2008, a conclave met in Dharamsala. It comprised around 300 people—Tibetans, leaders, intellectuals, activists, and representatives of Tibetans living across the world—who met within closed doors for five days. Kundun refused to participate in the discussions. He felt that the time had come for the people of Tibet to make their choice, either for complete independence or for genuine autonomy. He also refused to offer his comments, encouraging instead free speech from amongst his people. The conclave concluded that they would stand by Kundun's Middle Way policy. However, they also chose not to send any more delegations to Beijing, shifting the stand from a conciliatory approach to a more vocal demand for negotiations.

The conclave may not have provided for a dramatic turn of events, but it was evident that the Tibetan people still looked up to Kundun as their head of command. It was also evident that the struggle would not compromise on non-violence, as desired by their Kundun. Despite differences in opinion, Kundun was firmly acknowledged as the leader of the Tibetan people.

What would it mean for Tibet to have genuine autonomy?

According to Kundun's plan for genuine autonomy, the People's Republic of China can maintain foreign policy, defence and currency for Tibet. In return, Tibet will be allowed to retain her culture, language, religious practice, and all those factors that will protect her unique identity. He has also stated that under an autonomous rule, the education of Tibetan children will be planned and implemented by the Tibetans. The regional government will also manage the protection of the environment and natural resources.

Such autonomy would allow Tibetans to live independently within a larger Chinese governance without compromising their identity and culture.

Despite the repeated accusations and allegations, Kundun maintains a remarkable lack of anger and resentment towards the Chinese government. He has been called a 'demon', 'a wolf in monk's robes', even a thief and a murderer. Yet, he chooses to stay calm and not react. Asked often about his feelings towards the Chinese, he has never expressed any anger towards them. So much so, he goes on to add that he has nothing against the Chinese citizenry. He has repeatedly asked the Chinese people to 'use their eyes and ears' to decide for themselves what is the truth and what is distorted propaganda.

In a speech made at Stanford University, San Francisco, in 2010, he said, 'This century, whenever we face problems, we have to find ways through dialogue. The 200 million people murdered in the last century underscore the need for non-violence, mutual respect and compassion.'

The 17th Karmapa

On 5 January 2000, a taxi arrived in Dharamsala, very early in the morning. In the taxi was a fourteen-year old boy. He was the 17th Karmapa of Tibet, the third most influential figure in Tibet after the Dalai Lama and the Panchen Lama, and the head of the Kagyu sect of Tibetan Buddhism. The Karmapa had escaped from Tibet, evading the Chinese army, and entered India to seek asylum. His escape carried whiffs of an older memory, of Kundun's escape.

The Karmapa was born in 1985 to a nomadic family. His name at birth was Apo Gaga. The story goes that when Apo Gaga was around seven years old, he asked his family to move to another valley, and told them that some monks were expected to visit. The family agreed to shift, and sure enough were met by the followers of the 16th Karmapa who were searching for his reincarnation. They carried a letter where the 16th Karmapa had described and predicted his successor's birth, his qualities and where he would be found. Apo Gaga was found to match the predictions, and was brought to the Tsurphu Monastery, near Lhasa. With the approval of His Holiness the Dalai Lama, and with the permission of the Chinese government, Apo Gaga was enthroned as the 17th Karmapa on 27 September 1992. His ordained name was Ogyen Trinley Dorje.

As the 17th Karmapa, His Holiness Ogyen Trinley Dorje stayed at Tsurphu Monastery. With the passage of years, he felt he could no longer perform his duties under Chinese occupation. His teachers were all in exile in India. Eventually he decided to leave Tibet and thus began to plan his escape. On 28 December 1999, under cover of the night, the Karmapa left his monastery dressed as a civilian. People had been told that he was going into retreat and that his attendants, were going on a journey. The Karmapa, and one of his attendants, climbed out of his room, jumped on to the roof of a shrine, and from there to the ground, where a jeep waited, with a monk, Lama Tsultrim, and a driver. They were joined by two others, Lama Tsewang and a second driver. This group

drove night and day to arrive in Mustang, Nepal on 30 December 1999.

These were still the mountains to cross, which the Karmapa and his group passed on foot and horseback. They arrived in Manang, Nepal, from where, they travelled by helicopter and by car before arriving in Lucknow, India by train. Hiring a car in Lucknow, they made their way to Delhi and finally to Dharamsala. The first thing the Karmapa did was go see Kundun, who, he says, received him with great warmth and affection.

In exile, the Karmapa remains a revered leader among the Tibetans.

11　The Past, the Future and the Circle of Life

Lhamo Dhondup entered the Potala. Inside, he wandered into the chambers of the 13th Dalai Lama and looked at his possessions. 'My teeth', he declared, pointing to a set of dentures that had belonged to his predecessor. No one was surprised, for the boy had already indicated that he was the reincarnation of the 13th Dalai Lama.

Asked if he truly feels like the incarnation of the 13th Dalai Lama, Kundun says, 'My answer is Yes.' There are various differences between them but there are also a great many similarities. The Great Thirteenth was a man of foresight and vision. Kundun admits that it was a gift of clairvoyance or the ability to see events from the future that he himself does not possess. The Great Thirteenth was also a good politician, who actually started the process of Tibet's modernization. Kundun too believed that Tibet needed to accept change and modernity and had it not been for the untimely occupation of Tibet and his consequent exile, he would have continued his predecessor's ideas. Like his forerunner, he also shares a fascination for watches and rosaries!

Thomas Laird in his book *The Story of Tibet* says that between the 7th and 12th Dalai Lamas, there was a period of flux. Most of the Dalai Lamas died even before they reached adulthood. It rendered the institution of the Dalai Lama unstable and put the power of the country entirely in the hands of the Regent.

'I have never dreamed about them,' says Kundun about the 7th through the 12th Dalai Lamas. 'Only the Fifth Dalai Lama and the Thirteenth Dalai Lama have I dreamed of.' And in many ways, they are the Dalai Lamas whose work he has sought to continue.

In Mary Craig's biography of the Dalai Lama's family, the author reports that Kundun says that the 13th Dalai Lama had felt rather alone. And in this reincarnation, this loss seems to have been compensated for with Kundun's large family. His siblings have been strong allies, working closely with Kundun and deeply committed to the Tibetan struggle.

Among Kundun's sisters, Tsering Dolma took charge of the Tibetan refugee children soon after coming into exile. She set up the Tibetan Children's Village School and ran it until her untimely death in 1964. After that, Kundun's younger sister Jetsun Pema took over the administration of the school and the care of the children until as recently as 2006. She has also served in the Kashag as a Minister for Education, being the first woman minister in Tibet's history.

Three of Kundun's brothers have been monks, with Thubten Jigme Norbu and Tenzin Choegyal being recognized as *tulkus* or reincarnated high lamas. And yet, all three of them did give up their monastic lives subsequently. Thubten Jigme Norbu or Taktser

Rinpoche as he was better known, had left Tibet for exile soon after the Chinese invasion. He, along with Gyalo Dhondup, sought support for Tibet from the United States, believing that the superpower could help their cause. Taktser Rinpoche also worked for the exiled government before shifting to the United States. There, he founded the Tibetan Culture Center, and also served as Professor of Tibetan Studies at Indiana University. He passed away in 2008, and is survived by his wife and children.

Gyalo Dhondup has been among the most vocal of Tibetan supporters. In the 1950s, he sought the help of the United States government and was instrumental in the training of Tibetan guerrillas by the US Central Intelligence Agency (CIA). Later, he went on to serve the exiled government as the Kalon Tripa. He has been one of the key people to initiate talks with the Communist government. He now lives in Hong Kong.

Lobsang Samten was the closest companion of Kundun. He was known to be quiet, humble and peace-loving. Kundun remarks in his autobiography that Lobsang Samten once wept when he heard about a colony of lepers in Orissa and sought to help out wherever he could. His health, however, suffered several setbacks over the years and he died within five years of their mother's death, in 1981.

Tenzin Choegyal, Kundun's youngest sibling, was recognized as the reincarnate of a high monk called the Ngari Rinpoche. In exile, he renounced his monastic path. After graduating from college in 1969, he went on to work in the exile government. He has also served in the Tibetan regiment of the Indian army briefly, and has taught at the Tibetan Children's Village (TCV) schools. Tenzin Choegyal continues to live in Dharamsala with his wife and children.

Shortly after their mother's death, Kundun's brother Tenzin Choegyal met him and as they spoke, Choegyal remarked that he had once asked their mother who her favourite son was. To his surprise, she named Lobsang Samten. Tenzin Choegyal had assumed that as the youngest, he himself would be the undisputed favourite. And Kundun says that he had thought that she would have picked him to be her prefered choice.

The 15th Dalai Lama

Kundun's distance from politics has increased in the last decade with the creation and establishment of a democratic government in exile. He has voluntarily sought to step back from active politics, something that most of his people have resisted. For the Tibetan people, he still remains Tibet's ruler, the one who will protect them and lead them.

With every passing year, it has become increasingly important for Kundun to plan for life after him. The Buddha of Compassion has reincarnated when there was a need amongst people. Knowing that it is likely the Chinese government is waiting for his death to shake the struggle in its foundation, Kundun has actively sought to wean himself away from being the leader and allowing for a democratic establishment. He has publicly suggested that the incarnation of the Dalai Lama may end with him, and that 'the institution has outlived its usefulness.' More recently, he stated that the People's Republic of China might try to 'recognize' an incarnation themselves after him but there is no way the Dalai Lama will reincarnate in a country controlled by the Chinese government or in a country that is not free. In this regard the Chinese have set precedence with the Panchen Lama's reincarnation and sent out a message to the world. When the 10th Panchen Lama died, his reincarnation was recognized and approved by Kundun. However, the Chinese government overruled this decision, and appointed a boy they had chosen to be the next Panchen Lama. The original, Gedhun Choekyi Nyima, selected by Kundun, with his family were taken away and no one knows their whereabouts. It has been over a decade now and the Panchen Lama still remains in Chinese hands.

On 10 March 2011, the Tibetan National Uprising Day, Kundun issued a statement that made it to the headlines. With the Kalon Tripa elections only weeks away, Kundun stated that the time had come for Tibetans to have a leader elected by the people, one to whom he can pass on the temporal powers that he holds as the Dalai Lama. He went on to add that this does not mean that he will no longer work for Tibet. However, it is also important that people get used to being led by an elected leader.

Given this, it has become more and more imperative for the Tibetan government in exile to learn to exercise their powers of democracy, to be able to lead the people even in the absence of their God-King, and to continue negotiations and talks in order that they may one day return home to Tibet.

Towards Tibet

Within Tibet, people have been waiting for years for the Kundun to return. Often, children are sent to India by their parents, to go and live under the Dalai Lama's care. Exile offers the liberty to speak, to be educated, and most importantly for Tibetans, religious freedom. This means, however, that families are often separated because parents sometimes stay behind. Those who escape do so under threat of their lives. They must stay out of sight of the Chinese during their flight. They are not safe until they reach the Refugee Centre in Dharamsala. Once in Dharamsala, all new arrivals are granted an audience with Kundun, something Tibetans within Tibet can only dream of. In exile, they are rehabilitated, educated, and they live in settlements among their own people and preserve their own culture.

Yet, the constant question on every Tibetan's mind is when will the exile end. When will they return home, when can their Kundun return to Lhasa, to the Potala Palace, his rightful seat, which has remained unoccupied for sixty long years.

Kundun believes he will someday return to Tibet. The wait has been long and difficult. His people have waited with him, refusing to put down their roots in exile, ready to leave when it is time to go home again. Until that happens, their waiting continues.

Through all of this, through the uncertainty and difficulty of exile, what most people associate Kundun with is his easy laughter and affability. He continues to charm the world with it. In an interview given to journalist Glenn H. Mullin in 1987 he has said, 'I feel the Buddhist emphasis on love and patience has helped us considerably in coming through this difficult period of our history. It has helped us maintain a sense of clarity, strength and humour . . . the Tibetan people can still smile and laugh. They can still look to the future with eyes of hope. We call is *sem zangpo*—the good heart.'

A leader of the people, by the people, for the people

In the 2011 Kalon Tripa elections, the Tibetans in exile actually witnessed a democratic election process like they never had before. Three men were nominated for the post. Their names were Lobsang Sangay, Tenzin Tethong and Tashi Wangdi. Just before the elections, Kundun had announced that the representative elected by the people as Kalon Tripa would be handed over all the temporal duties vested all this while in the Dalai Lama.

Historically, the Kalon Tripa has always been selected by Kundun and remained answerable to him. But now, the Kalon Tripa would function as the political head of the Tibetan people. He, in turn, would elect the seven members to his cabinet or Kashag. The Ministers are called Kalons and head the various departments of Education, Finance, Health, Home, Religion and Culture, Security, Information and International Relations.

The 2011 Kalon Tripa elections were won by Lobsang Sangay, the youngest candidate. A lawyer who has been educated at Harvard University in the United States, Sangay won by 55 per cent of the votes. What is quite interesting also is that for the first time since the 5th Dalai Lama, that a layman and not a monk has become the leader of the Tibetan people.

Lobsang Sangay's work is not going to be easy. He is now the leader of a people without a country. He heads a government that no country will recognize. At best, the Tibetan government in Dharamsala is recognized as an exiled administration with Lobsang Sangay at its head. The Tibetans in exile in thirty countries look to him as their leader. The Tibetans within Tibet look to him as the man who can bring about change after half a century of oppression. The Chinese government refuses to recognize his leadership.

Lobsang Sangay, however, is a man of determination. He has chosen to carry on the work of Kundun by advocating non-violence while seeking genuine autonomy for Tibet. He also vows to take Kundun someday back to the Potala Palace in Lhasa.

TRIVIA
TREASURY

Turn the pages to discover more fascinating facts and tantalizing tidbits of history about this legendary life and his world.

WHAT HAPPENED AND WHEN

Some momentous events that took place in the world during the time of the 14th Dalai Lama:

- **1935**: Persia officially renamed as Iran.
- **1935**: Mussolini of Italy invades Ethiopia.
- **1936**: Civil war in Spain.
- **1939**: World War II begins.
- **1940**: Mahatma Gandhi writes to Adolf Hitler requesting him to stop the war.
- **1941**: Japan attacks Pearl Harbour.
- **1945**: World War II ends. United Nations formed.
- **1947**: Partition of India and Pakistan.
- **1948**: Mahatma Gandhi assassinated.
- **1948**: Burma freed from the British.
- **1949**: China under Mao Tse Tung invades East Turkestan.
- **1950**: *The Diary of Anne Frank* published.
- **1950–53**: War between North and South Korea.
- **1952**: King George VI of Britain dies. He is succeeded by Princess Elizabeth, who reigns even today.
- **1955**: The Vietnam War begins.

- **1956**: The States Reorganization Act passed in India.
- **The '60s**: Thirty-two African countries gain independence from European colonial powers.
- **1961**: The Berlin Wall comes up dividing Germany into a Communist East and a Democratic West.
- **1963**: Martin Luther King Jr. delivers his famous speech—'I have a dream…'
- **1963**: United States President John F. Kennedy assassinated.
- **1972**: Palestinian terrorists kidnap and murder eleven Israeli athletes at the Summer Olympics in Munich.
- **1979**: War between the Soviet Union and the *mujahideen* in Afghanistan.
- **1980**: War between Iran and Iraq begins.
- **1982**: Canada becomes independent.
- **The '80s**: Military dictatorship comes to an end in Brazil, Argentina, Chile and Uruguay. Democratic government formed.
- **1984**: Indian Prime Minister Indira Gandhi assassinated in New Delhi.
- **1985**: Mikhail Gorbachev becomes the leader of the Soviet Union.
- **1990**: Nelson Mandela released after thirty years of imprisonment.
- **1990**: The Berlin Wall is brought down and Germany of reunited.
- **1991**: Indian Prime Minister Rajiv Gandhi is assassinated.
- **1992**: The Euro, a common currency, created for the countries of the European Union.

- **1993**: Palestine and Israel sign a peace treaty facilitated by the US President Bill Clinton.
- **1999**: Pakistan's Army Chief Pervez Musharraf seizes power in a military coup, ousting Prime Minister Nawaz Sharief.
- **The 2000s**: South America sees a return to Communism with Left wing parties rising to power in Bolivia, Paraguay, Venezuela and Ecuador.
- **2001**: Osama Bin Laden's Al Qaeda attack the World Trade Centre in New York.
- **2002**: The International Criminal Court was formed to prosecute individuals for crimes against humanity.
- **2006**: In Nepal, monarchy comes to an end. Elections held. The Communist Party of Nepal comes to power.
- **2008**: Terrorist attacks in Mumbai by Pakistan-based terror group Lashkar-e-Taiba.
- **2009**: The Sri Lankan Civil War between the Sri Lankan army and the Tamil rebels ends after twenty-five years.
- **2009**: Barack Obama sworn in as US President. For the first time, an African American occupies this seat in the history of the United States.

CHRONOLOGY OF EVENTS IN TIBETAN HISTORY

- **620–649 AD**: The reign of Songtsen Gampo, probably the most famous of Tibetan kings. During this time Buddhism was introduced.

- **754–797** AD: Tibet was ruled by Trisong Detsen who conquered China. During his reign, the first monastery, Samye, was built in Tibet at Dranang.
- **1073** AD: The Sakya monastery was founded by Konchog Gyalpo, whose son founded the Sakya sect.
- **1207** AD: Genghis Khan assumed power. His rule included China, Korea and Tibet. His grandson Kublai Khan converted to Tibetan Buddhism in 1270.
- **1357** AD: Tsongkhapa Dragpa, the greatest of the Tibetan scholars and the founder of the Gelug sect, was born.
- **1416**: Pema Dorjee was ordained as Gedun Drupa and became the first Dalai Lama.
- **1578** AD: The third incarnation of Gedun Drupa, Sonam Gyatso, was conferred the title Dalai Lama, by the Mongolian prince Altan Khan.
- **1642**: The 5th Dalai Lama assumed spiritual and temporal power of Tibet. During his reign China recognized Tibet as an independent country.
- **1720** AD: The Manchu army entered Lhasa.
- **1723–35** AD: Emperor Kangxi assumed power in China, and withdrew troops from Lhasa.
- **1788** AD: Nepal invaded Tibet. China came to Tibet's assistance and a peace treaty was signed.
- **1795** AD: The decline of the Qing dynasty in China began. Tibet sought to regain her freedom.
- **1854** AD: Nepal invaded Tibet again and in the absence of Chinese intervention, a treaty was signed between the two countries.

- **1895 AD**: The 13th Dalai Lama assumed power.
- **1903 AD**: A British expedition attacked and defeated the Tibetan Army. Dalai Lama sought asylum in Mongolia.
- **1904 AD**: The British withdrew from Tibet after the Lhasa Convention signed between the two countries.
- **1909 AD**: The 13th Dalai Lama sought exile in India following Manchu invasion. He stayed for three years until the fall of the Qing dynasty in China in 1911. Following this, the Chinese troops withdrew from Tibet. The Republic of China was formed.
- **1912 AD**: The Tibetan government ordered all Chinese to leave Tibet.
- **1913 AD**: The 13th Dalai Lama and the Tibetan National Assembly proclaimed Tibet's independence.
- **1914 AD**: Great Britain, China and Tibet met in Simla, India. The agreement was that Tibet was to be divided into Inner and Outer Tibet. Inner Tibet was under Chinese suzerainty while its administration was managed by the government in Lhasa. China refused to sign the treaty.
- **1933 AD**: The 13th Dalai Lama passed away.

IMPORTANT DATES IN THE TIBETAN CALENDAR

- **Feb–Mar**: Losar, the Tibetan New Year
- **March**: Monlam or the Great Prayer festival
- **10 March**: National Uprising Day

- **15 April**: Saka Dawa, the birth of Buddha or the Sakyamuni
- **6 July**: Kundun's birthday, now celebrated as World Tibet Day, in order to highlight the cause of Tibet's freedom. It was first celebrated in 1998. The objective is to garner support and awareness for the Tibetan cause, while also celebrating Tibet's unique culture.

SOME ASPECTS OF TIBETAN CULTURE

The *lungta* prayer flag or the 'Wind Horse' comes in five colours—blue, white, red, green, yellow—corresponding to the five elements sky, wind, fire, water and earth. On these coloured squares are prayers. The Tibetans tie these prayer flags so that the wind can carry the prayers and spread its good fortune everywhere.

The prayer wheel is a large cylindrical drum-like object with the Tibetan prayer 'Om Mani Padme Hum' carved on it. The wheel is turned to rotate in the clockwise direction. Tibetan Buddhists believe that turning the prayer wheel is a way to earn good *karma*.

A *khata* is a silk scarf with auspicious symbols, and used to seek blessings from high lamas, for greeting people at weddings and birth, even death.

TENZINS IN EXILE

In Tibet, tradition has it that when a child is born, the parents approach a lama for a name. The naming convention includes two names and there is no concept of a surname or family name. Tibetans also change names during their lives at various points, after a serious illness or in the face of calamity or after marriage. There is nothing unusual about it.

The Tibetans in exile have access to Kundun and many parents go to him for a name for their newborn. The names that Kundun gives always begin with 'Tenzin', which comes from his own name—Tenzin Gyatso. 'Tenzin' has thus become the most common name in exile and both boys and girls have it in their names. As some of them say, the name 'Tenzin' is an added indication of their loyalty and closeness to the Dalai Lama.

KUNDUN AND HIS PETS

Kundun has always enjoyed the company of animals, growing up as he did in the Norbulingka with its large garden and all those animals and birds and fishes. In Dharamsala, Kundun had two dogs, Tashi and Sangye.

He once also adopted a stray cat and named her Tsering. Now Tsering proved to be the ideal pet, obedient and loyal to Kundun. Her one flaw, he says, was that she couldn't resist chasing mice. And Kundun could not bear to see her kill them. Once, when he caught her chasing a mouse, he went after Tsering, who knew she had done something wrong. She ran up a curtain and in the process fell down, injuring her leg badly. Full of remorse, Kundun tended to her but she did not recover from the injury and died within a few days.

Some weeks later, Kundun heard a pitiful cry in his garden. When he went to check, he found an abandoned kitten lying in the bushes. The kitten was also crippled, exactly as Tsering had been. Kundun took her in and tended to her. She became part of the household, along with Tashi and Sangye. But, Kundun says, given a choice, he would not have a pet for he finds that animals too, like people, when left to themselves, choose freedom.

DALAI LAMA ONLINE

Kundun is among the most accessible of world leaders. From being god reincarnate in the formidable Potala Palace to the monk in exile who welcomes every single countryman, he has personified the practice of democracy. His days are packed with public and private audiences. The Office of His Holiness the Dalai Lama provides information on his schedule and his teachings on a regularly updated website (www.dalailama.com) and takes care of his correspondence. Kundun has always been fascinated with machines and how they work from his childhood and new technologies like the Internet are now very much a part of his life. Webcast interviews, online updates and of course, Twitter (where he has over two million followers) are the various ways that he stays connected with people the world over.

DHARAMSALA—LITTLE LHASA IN INDIA

Dharamsala, in the Indian state of Himachal Pradesh, is today the most important centre for the Tibetan people. Its attractions are several, from trekking trails to rock climbing, from Tibetan food like *momos* and *thukpas* to Italian cafes serving pizzas and pasta and freshly baked bread.

The best way to travel to Dharamsala is by bus or train from Delhi. It's an overnight journey. Once you reach here, head for Upper Dharamsala where the Tibetan community lives. Places to visit are the Norbulingka Institute, which houses a Doll Museum, a temple and a beautiful garden. The Institute works towards preserving Tibetan arts and culture. The Tibetan Institute of Performing Arts organizes performances of Tibetan dance and drama which are worth looking out for. The Tibetan New Year of Losar which falls in Feb–March every year is a great time to see Tibetan culture at its fullest here.

Dharmasala is a place that offers a very rich cultural experience with its monasteries and arts and people. But above all, the biggest attraction here is the Dalai Lama. It is Dharamasala that he has called his home for a good half century. Here he gives private and public audiences and media interviews. He meets every single Tibetan who arrives from Tibet, inquires into their well being and makes sure that they are taken good care of. Occasionally, he joins the crowds to watch an IPL cricket match or even football, which is a more popular sport with the Tibetans.

Dharamsala today is so synonymous with the Tibetan community that it's often referred to as 'Little Lhasa'. In fact, the locals often refer to it as Dhasa, a shortening of 'Dharamsala' and so similar to 'Lhasa'. And that in many ways is what the town of Dharamsala is—a little bit of what Lhasa was and so many other things that it was not.

BOOKS AUTHORED BY THE DALAI LAMA

Here are some of his autobiographies and memoirs

My Land and My People
Freedom in Exile
My Spiritual Journey

He has also written several books on Tibetan Buddhism, Philosophy as well as books on finding peace and happiness despite the stress of modern living.

BOOKS TO READ

Here are some books you can read if you wish to find out more about the Dalai Lama.

1. *Dalai Lama, A Biography of the Tibetan Spiritual and Political Leader* by Demi (Henry Holt and Co., 1998)

2. *The 14th Dalai Lama: A Manga Biography* by Tetsu Sawai, (Emotional Content, 2008)

3. *Seven Years in Tibet* by Heinrich Harrer (Harper Collins India, 2005)

4. *Kundun: A Biography of the Family of the Dalai Lama* by Mary Craig (Harper Collins Publishers, 1997)

5. *Dalai Lama, My Son: A Mother's Story* by Deki Tsering (Penguin Books India, 2001)

6. *Caravan to Tibet* by Deepa Agarwal (Puffin India, 2007)

7. *My Land and My People, Memoirs of His Holiness, the Dalai Lama* (Srishti Publishers & Distributors, 1997)

8. *Freedom in Exile, The Autobiography of the Dalai Lama of Tibet*, (Hodder and Stoughton Ltd., 1990)